FAST FACTS

**Indispensable
Guides to
Clinical
Practice**

Schizophrenia

Professor of Adult Psychiatry,
University of Manchester,
Manchester, UK

Robert W Buchanan

Chief, Outpatient Research Program,
Maryland Psychiatric Research Center,
Department of Psychiatry, University of
Maryland School of Medicine, Baltimore,
Maryland, USA

HEALTH PRESS

Oxford

Fast Facts – Schizophrenia
First published 1998
Reprinted 2000
Second edition September 2002

Text © 2002 Shôn W Lewis, Robert W Buchanan
© 2002 in this edition Health Press Limited
Health Press Limited, Elizabeth House, Queen Street,
Abingdon, Oxford OX14 3JR, UK
Tel: +44 (0)1235 523233
Fax: +44 (0)1235 523238

Fast Facts is a trademark of Health Press Limited.

The publisher and the authors have made every effort to ensure the
accuracy of this book, but cannot accept responsibility for any errors or
omissions.

A CIP catalogue record for this title is available from the British Library.

ISBN 1-903734-24-X

Lewis, SW (Shôn)
Fast Facts – Schizophrenia/
Shôn W Lewis, Robert W Buchanan

Typesetting and page layout by Zed, Oxford, UK.

Printed by Fine Print (Services) Limited, Oxford, UK.

Glossary

AMPA: α-amino-3-hydroxy-5-methyl-4-isoxazole propionic acid, a glutamatergic neurotransmitter

BOLD imaging: blood-oxygen-level-dependent imaging. This magnetic resonance imaging technique uses the natural paramagnetic properties of hemoglobin as it deoxygenates to produce an image of regional cerebral blood flow

CBT: cognitive–behavior therapy

CPZE: chlorpromazine equivalents

CSF: cerebrospinal fluid

CT: computed tomography

DTI: diffusion tensor imaging, a type of MRI allowing visualization of white matter tracts

DUP: duration of untreated psychosis

DZ: dizygotic (of two fertilized eggs); dizygotic twins are non-identical

EPS: extrapyramidal side-effects, e.g. akinesia, dystonia, akathisia and tremor

fMR: functional magnetic resonance, a means of imaging based on the same principles as BOLD imaging

GPI: general paresis of the insane

MRI: magnetic resonance imaging

MZ: monozygotic (of one fertilized egg); monozygotic twins are identical

NGA: new-generation antipsychotic, a class of drugs available since 1990, including clozapine; broadly synonymous with 'atypical' antipsychotic

NMDA: N-methyl-D-aspartate

NMS: neuroleptic malignant syndrome, a syndrome characterized by muscle rigidity, autonomic instability, fever and mental status changes

PEG: pneumoencephalography, an old imaging technique based on the x-ray contrast of air injected into the lumbar subarachnoid space, bone and brain tissue

PET: positron emission tomography, a functional imaging technique used to measure either glucose metabolism, regional cerebral blood flow, or receptor occupancy

Potency: how much of a drug is needed to have an effect

rCBF: regional cerebral blood flow

SPET: single-photon emission tomography, another functional imaging technique based on principles similar to PET. SPET is less versatile than PET

STG: superior temporal gyrus

TD: tardive dyskinesia, a major side-effect associated with all conventional antipsychotics. It is characterized by abnormal, involuntary movements and primarily affects the muscles of the tongue and face, but may also involve the muscles of the extremities, pelvic girdle and/or the diaphragm

VCFS: velocardiofacial syndrome

Introduction

At the beginning of the 21st century, schizophrenia remains one of the major public health challenges. Recent advances in research have given tantalizing clues as to its causes. New drug and non-drug treatments hold prospects of better clinical and social outcomes. In the second edition of *Fast Facts – Schizophrenia*, we review what is new and promising in the understanding of risk factors, symptoms, cognitive and brain deficits, and treatment strategies.

Pre-classical and classical descriptions

The earliest descriptions of symptoms associated with the diagnosis of schizophrenia date back to pre-classical cultures. Such symptoms were then considered to be the manifestions of supernatural forces invading the individual, often as punishment for immoral behavior. In ancient Greece and Rome, the focus for studying and understanding mental illnesses moved towards a naturalistic standpoint. Early Greek physicians described delusions of grandeur, paranoia and deterioration in cognitive functions and personality. These behaviors were attributed generally to disturbances among the relationships of the four bodily humors: blood, yellow bile, black bile and phlegm.

Medieval times

In medieval times, particularly in Western societies, there was a return to the pre-classical moralistic or superstitious perspectives of psychotic behavior. The classical models of illness were largely kept alive by Arabic physicians, who practiced medicine according to the ideas of Hippocrates, Aristotle and Galen. These classical conceptualizations of psychosis went unchanged until the Renaissance.

The Renaissance

In Western cultures, the Renaissance led to a re-emergence of interest in classical thought, with a reawakening of the conceptualization of mental illnesses, including psychoses, as naturalistic disorders. The first European psychiatric hospitals were established during this period. The 17th and 18th centuries saw an explosion of information about the workings of the body, which led to a more rational and scientific approach to diseases and the study of the mind. Organic etiologies of mental illness were adopted, and the initial descriptions and classifications of these disorders were attempted.

19th century

In the first part of the 19th century, the foundations for the modern concept of schizophrenia were established (Table 1.1). An early diagnostic system emerged and various mental illnesses were described, including epilepsy, melancholia, mania and the dementing psychotic disorders, which included schizophrenia and general paresis of the

TABLE 1.1

Major landmarks in the development of the concept of schizophrenia

Haslam J, 1809	Published treatise on a type of insanity that occurs in the young
Esquirol JED, 1838	Described the prognosis and long-term course of different forms of insanity
Morel BA, 1860	Described 'démence précoce,' a progressive deterioration evolving quickly in young persons
Kahlbaum KL, 1863	Described a form of insanity characterized by abnormal posturing, 'catatonia'
Hecker E, 1871	Described a form of insanity characterized by onset in puberty, evolution through successive affective states, ultimately resulting in states of psychological weakness and mental deficiency, 'hebephrenia'
Kraepelin E, 1898–99	Grouped together as a single illness dementia praecox and the formerly separate entities hebephrenia, catatonia and paranoid psychosis. Distinguished dementia praecox from manic–depressive illness on the basis of disease course and long-term outcome
Bleuler E, 1911	Recognized that patients with dementia praecox did not always deteriorate, coined the term schizophrenia and described fundamental symptoms
Kasanin J, 1933	Introduced the concept of schizoaffective disorder
Langfeldt G, 1939	Introduced the concept of schizophreniform disorder
Schneider K, 1946 (translated 1959)	Proposed the existence of pathognomonic, or first-rank, symptoms

insane (GPI). However, a general approach that could integrate the diverse manifestations of mental illness into distinct clinical syndromes was lacking. The situation was complicated by the overlap in the clinical presentation of these disorders. Furthermore, the clinical presentation of an individual could change over time, and patients with the same symptoms could have different outcomes.

20th century

Two developments led to the eventual delineation of schizophrenia from the other dementing psychoses. First, the limitations of cross-sectional descriptions of symptoms for classifying mental disorders led to the emergence of a new system based on unified causes, clinicopathological correlations and the longitudinal course and prognosis of presumed disorders. The other development was the identification of the spirochete as the causal agent in GPI (Figure 1.1). In the 19th century, GPI was a common form of insanity. Its symptom manifestations were diverse and overlapped extensively with schizophrenic symptomatology. The identification of GPI as syphilitic insanity helped Emil Kraepelin (Figure 1.2) to delineate the

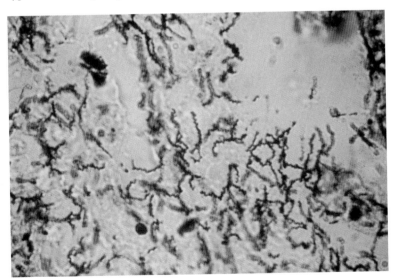

Figure 1.1 The spirochete, identified as the agent causing a major 19th-century mental illness, general paresis of the insane.

Figure 1.2 Emil Kraepelin, the German psychiatrist who identified dementia praecox (schizophrenia). His students included Alzheimer.

two other major patterns of insanity: manic–depressive psychosis and dementia praecox (or dementia of the young: schizophrenia), and to group together under the heading of dementia praecox the previously disparate categories of insanity, including hebephrenia, paranoia and catatonia.

In differentiating dementia praecox from manic–depressive disorder, Kraepelin emphasized the early onset and what he believed to be the inevitable deteriorating course of dementia praecox, compared with the relatively good outcome of manic–depressive illness. Kraepelin also described what he thought were the two main pathological processes occurring in patients with schizophrenia:

'On the one hand we observe a weakening of those emotional activities which permanently form the mainsprings of volition ... mental activity and instinct for occupation become mute. The result of this part of the process is emotional dullness, failure of mental activities, loss of mastery over volition, of endeavor, and of ability for independent action. The essence of personality is thereby destroyed, the best and most precious part of its being, as Griesinger once expressed it, torn from her ...

The second group of disorders ... consists in the loss of the inner unity of the activities of intellect, emotion, and volition in themselves and among one another. Stransky speaks of an annihilation of the "intrapsychic co-ordination" ... this annihilation presents itself to us in the disorders of association described by Bleuler, in incoherence of the train of thought, in the sharp change of moods as well as in desultoriness and derailments in practical work ... the near connections between thinking and feeling, between deliberation and emotional activity on the one hand, and practical work on the other is more or less lost. Emotions do not correspond to ideas.' (*Dementia Praecox and Paraphrenia*, 1919)

The former process corresponds to our current concept of the negative symptoms, and the latter to the positive symptoms of schizophrenia.

In 1911, Eugen Bleuler (Figure 1.3), recognizing that dementia was not a necessary characteristic of dementia praecox, suggested the term 'schizophrenia' (splitting of the mind) for the disorder. Bleuler believed that schizophrenia represented a syndrome consisting of several disorders that shared a common psychopathology. He also introduced the concept of primary and secondary schizophrenic symptoms; his four primary symptoms (the four As) were:

- abnormal associations
- autistic behavior and thinking
- abnormal affect
- ambivalence.

Of these four symptoms, Bleuler viewed as central to the illness the loss of association between thought processes, and that between thought, emotion and behavior.

Since Kraepelin and Bleuler, there have been relatively few modifications of the concept of schizophrenia. The concepts of schizophreniform and schizoaffective disorder were introduced in the 20th century, but these largely represent refinements in the boundary between schizophrenia and the affective disorders.

Figure 1.3 Eugen Bleuler, the Swiss psychiatrist who coined the term 'schizophrenia'. His students included Jung.

Schizophrenia today

Currently, schizophrenia has the status of a syndrome resulting from multiple causal pathways. These pathways involve disorders of normal brain function, which give rise to characteristic symptoms and functional impairments. These manifestations and their long-term course differentiate schizophrenia from other forms of psychosis.

A brief history – Key points

- Schizophrenia was first clearly identified in the 1890s.
- Its characteristic features were an early onset and a chronic course.

Key references

Bleuler E. *Dementia Praecox or the Group of Schizophrenias (1911).* Translated by Zinken J. New York: International Universities Press, 1950.

Howells JG, ed. *The Concept of Schizophrenia: Historical Perspectives.* Washington DC: American Psychiatric Press, 1991.

Kraepelin E. *Dementia Praecox and Paraphrenia.* Translated by Barclay RM. Huntington, WV: Robert E Krieger., 1971.

Current diagnostic criteria

Whether or not schizophrenia can be classified as a disease has been much debated. Strictly speaking, schizophrenia is a syndrome – a disorder for which there is no objective test or pathology, but which is identified by a characteristic cluster of symptoms that last for a certain time. In the 1930s, Kurt Schneider reviewed many case records and listed eight symptoms that he considered diagnostic of schizophrenia. These specific types of delusions and hallucinations became known as 'Schneider's first-rank symptoms' (Table 2.1), although they also occur occasionally in other serious psychiatric disorders.

The loosening of the diagnostic boundaries in schizophrenia became a concern in the early 1970s. A series of studies showed that clinicians

TABLE 2.1

Schneider's first-rank symptoms of schizophrenia

Thought insertion, withdrawal or broadcasting	The experience of one's thoughts being put into or taken out of one's head, or broadcast to others. Collectively known as 'thought interference'
Passivity experiences	Experience that one's thoughts or actions are physically being controlled by an external force: 'made actions'
Delusional perception	A normal perception followed suddenly by a seemingly unrelated, fully formed delusion. Rare
Echo de la pensée	Hallucination of a voice repeating one's own thoughts
Running commentary	Hallucination describing one's current actions
Third-person auditory hallucinations	Voices describing patient as 'he' or 'she'

varied widely in their diagnosis of schizophrenia, which was made twice as often in North America as in Europe. As a result, operational diagnostic criteria, such as the Research Diagnostic Criteria of Endicott and Spitzer, were developed, initially for use in research, to try to standardize diagnosis. This approach gives a menu of possible symptoms and specifies that a certain number should be present for a minimum duration before a diagnosis can be made.

Since 1994, the two main classification systems in use worldwide are DSM-IV, developed by the American Psychiatric Association, and ICD-10, developed by the World Health Organization and mainly used outside North America. In their definitions of schizophrenia, the two systems are similar (Tables 2.2 and 2.3). Both diagnose schizophrenia with inter-rater reliabilities of at least 0.8, which compares well with many other medical disorders. Each specifies the presence of one first-rank-type symptom, or two symptoms from a list of positive and negative symptoms. The main differences are that DSM-IV states a minimum duration of symptoms, including prodromal symptoms, for 6 months, and also includes deterioration of social functioning. ICD-10 specifies just 1 month of symptoms. A classification of an acute form of schizophrenia in ICD-10 is equivalent to a classification of schizophreniform disorder in DSM-IV. These differences mean that DSM-IV schizophrenia has a lower incidence and prevalence than ICD-10 schizophrenia, and has a worse prognosis as a result of the degree of chronicity in its definition. As there is a slight tendency for schizophrenia to be more chronic in men than women, the sex ratio shows a male predominance for DSM-IV schizophrenia that is less apparent in ICD-10.

The core symptoms

A large number of studies have found that the symptoms of schizophrenia usually segregate into three semi-independent symptom complexes (Table 2.4). The three-syndrome model was first proposed in the 1980s and has been confirmed in subsequent studies. The presence and severity of negative symptoms are more critical to the prognosis than the positive symptom complexes; negative symptoms include blunted, abnormally unresponsive mood, reduced willpower, reduced

TABLE 2.2

DSM-IV diagnostic criteria for schizophrenia

A. *Characteristic symptoms:* two (or more) of the following, each present for a significant portion of time during a 1-month period (or less if successfully treated):
   (1) delusions
   (2) hallucinations
   (3) disorganized speech (e.g. frequent derailment or incoherence)
   (4) grossly disorganized or catatonic behavior
   (5) negative symptoms (i.e. affective flattening, alogia, or avolition)
   Note: only one criterion A symptom is required if delusions are bizarre or hallucinations consist of a voice keeping up a running commentary on the person's behavior or thoughts, or two or more voices conversing with each other.

B. *Social/occupational dysfunction:* for a significant portion of the time since the onset of the disturbance, one or more major areas of functioning, such as work, interpersonal relations, or self-care, are markedly below the level achieved prior to the onset (or when the onset is in childhood or adolescence, failure to achieve expected level of interpersonal, academic or occupational achievement).

C. *Duration:* continuous signs of the disturbance persist for at least 6 months. This 6-month period must include at least 1 month of symptoms (or less if successfully treated) that meet criterion A (i.e. active-phase symptoms) and may include periods of prodromal or residual symptoms. During these prodromal or residual periods, the signs of the disturbance may be manifested by only negative symptoms or two or more symptoms listed in criterion A present in an attenuated form (e.g. odd beliefs, unusual perceptual experiences).

D. *Schizoaffective and mood disorder exclusion:* schizoaffective disorder and mood disorder with psychotic features have been ruled out because either (1) no major depressive, manic or mixed episodes have occurred concurrently with the active-phase symptoms; or (2) if mood episodes have occurred during active-phase symptoms, their total duration has been brief relative to the duration of the active and residual periods.

E. *Substance / general medical condition exclusion:* the disturbance is not due to the direct physiological effects of a substance (e.g. a drug of abuse, a medication) or a general medical condition.

F. *Relationship to a pervasive development disorder:* if there is a history of autistic disorder or another pervasive development disorder, the additional diagnosis of schizophrenia is made only if prominent delusions or hallucinations are also present for at least 1 month (or less if successfully treated).

Reproduced, with permission, from American Psychiatric Association 1994

TABLE 2.3

ICD-10 diagnostic criteria

(a) Thought echo, thought insertion or withdrawal, or thought broadcasting

(b) Delusions of control, influence or passivity, clearly referred to body or limb movements or specific thoughts, actions or sensations; delusional perception

(c) Hallucinatory voices giving a running commentary on the patient's behavior, or discussing the patient among themselves, or other types of hallucinatory voices coming from some part of the body

(d) Persistent delusions of other kinds that are culturally inappropriate and completely impossible (e.g. being able to control the weather, or being in communication with aliens from another world)

(e) Persistent hallucinations in any modality, when accompanied either by fleeting or half-formed delusions without clear affective content, or by persistent over-valued ideas, or when occurring every day for weeks or months on end

(f) Breaks or interpolations in the train of thought, resulting in incoherence or irrelevant speech, or neologisms

(g) Catatonic behavior, such as excitement, posturing, or waxy flexibility, negativism, mutism and stupor

(h) 'Negative' symptoms, such as marked apathy, paucity of speech, and blunting or incongruity of emotional responses; it must be clear that these are not due to depression or to neuroleptic medication

Diagnostic guidelines

The normal requirement for a diagnosis of schizophrenia is that a minimum of one clear symptom (and usually two or more if less clear-cut) belonging to any one of the groups listed as (a) to (d) above, or symptoms from at least two of the groups referred to as (e) to (h), should have been clearly present for most of the time *during a period of 1 month or more*.

Adapted, with permission, from World Health Organization 1993

amount of spontaneous speech, and loss of self-care skills. Negative symptoms can become progressively more severe and often persist to a degree even when positive symptoms have improved. It is important to distinguish between primary negative symptoms, which are indisputably part of the illness, and secondary negative symptoms. The latter can be similar in quality but result from a superimposed anxious or depressed mood, an impoverished, understimulating environment or the side-effects of antipsychotic medication.

The third symptom complex, disorganized behavior, refers to a disruption in the associations among affect, thought and behavior. Inappropriate affect is the loss of connection between affect and thought (e.g. the patient who laughs while talking about the death of a loved one). Positive formal thought disorder is a disruption of the normal grammatical and syntactic use of conversational language, such that statements become connected in unusual ways ('knights-move thinking'); words are used idiosyncratically (paraphasia) or invented words used (neologisms); or speech is rambling with little information content (poverty of speech content). Bizarre behavior refers to the socially inappropriate or disorganized behavior frequently exhibited by patients with schizophrenia.

Rating scales

Symptom rating allows us to track clinical change over time and to assess outcome. It is an increasingly important function in service and treatment evaluation. Outcome of schizophrenia can be measured in terms of severity of symptoms, or social outcome, or by related

TABLE 2.4

The three-syndrome model of schizophrenia*

Syndrome	Symptom pattern
1 Reality distortion	Delusions
	Auditory hallucinations
2 Psychomotor poverty	Poverty of speech
	Blunted affect
	Decreased spontaneous movement
3 Disorganization	Formal thought disorder
	Inappropriate affect

*Terminology after Liddle 1987

TABLE 2.5

Measurable dimensions of outcome in schizophrenia and the most widely used rating scales

Outcome	Scale
Symptoms	Brief Psychiatric Rating Scale
	SAPS, SANS (Scales for the Assessment of Positive/Negative Symptoms)[1]
	Positive and Negative Syndrome Scale (PANSS)[2]
Social functioning/ behavior/adjustment	Social Functioning Scale[3]
	Social Behavior Schedule[4]
Global functioning	Global Assessment of Functioning (in DSM-IV)[5]
Quality of life	Quality of Life Interview (US version: Lehmann 1988; UK version: Oliver 1993)
	Quality-of-Life Scale[6]
Satisfaction with services	General Satisfaction Questionnaire[7]
Use of services	Hospital inpatient days
Occupational	Days in work

1 Andreasen 1989
2 Kay et al. 1987
3 Birchwood et al. 1990
4 Wykes and Sturt 1986
5 Jones et al. 1995
6 Heinrichs et al. 1984
7 Huxley and Mohamad 1991

constructs such as quality of life or patient satisfaction (Table 2.5). The characteristics to look for in a rating scale are listed in Table 2.6.

The Positive and Negative Syndrome Scale (PANSS) is now the most widely used of the symptom rating scales. It comprises three subscales which rate positive, negative and general symptoms, respectively. It takes about 20 minutes to administer. Symptomatic patients score typically between 60 and 120, and a score reduction of 20% is clinically useful.

TABLE 2.6

What are the characteristics to look for in a rating scale?

- Logical and understandable
- Relevant to the study population
- Proven validity (measures what it claims to measure)
- Proven reliability, between raters and over time
- Sensitivity to change
- Availability of training and manuals/video

Social functioning is a less frequently measured, but very important, outcome. The Social Behavior Schedule (SBS) is probably the best instrument, though it needs to involve a caregiver.

Global functioning can be estimated very simply using the Global Assessment of Functioning (GAF). Based on anchor points, this gives a single score from 0 to 100 depending on how the person is functioning in general.

Quality of life is an increasingly important concept, but the best way of measuring it is controversial. The Quality-of-Life Scale (QLS) is probably the most widely used schizophrenia-specific scale.

Symptoms and diagnoses – Key points

- Positive symptoms such as delusions and hallucinations in schizophrenia can be assessed reliably.
- Negative symptoms have greater prognostic importance.
- A third cluster of symptoms in schizophrenia comprises disorganized speech and behavior.
- It is important to rate social and behavioral outcomes as well as symptoms.

Key references

American Psychiatric Association. *Diagnostic and Statistical Manual of Mental Disorders*, 4th edn *(DSM-IV)*. Washington DC: American Psychiatric Press, 1994.

Andreason NC. The scale for assessing negative symptoms (SANS): conceptual and theoretical foundations. *Br J Psychiatry* 1989;155(suppl 7):49–52.

Birchwood M, Smith T, Cochrane R et al. The Social Functioning Scale: a new scale of social adjustment for use in family intervention programmes with schizophrenic patients. *Br J Psychiatry* 1990;157:853–9.

Crow TJ. Positive and negative schizophrenic symptoms and the role of dopamine. *Br J Psychiatry* 1980;137:282.

Heinrichs D, Hanlon TE, Carpenter WT. The quality of life scale. *Schizophr Bull* 1984;10:388–96.

Huxley P, Mohamad H. The development of a General Satisfaction Questionnaire for program evaluation. *Soc Work Soc Sci Rev* 1991;14:63–74.

Jones S, Thornicroft G, Coffey M, Dunn G. A brief mental health outcome scale: reliability and validity of the GAF. *Br J Psychiatry* 1995;166:654–9.

Kay SR, Fishbein A, Opler LA. The positive and negative syndrome scale (PANSS) for schizophrenia. *Schizophr Bull* 1987;13:261–76.

Kendell RE, Cooper JE, Gourlay AG. Diagnostic criteria of American and British psychiatrists. *Arch Gen Psychiatry* 1971;25:123–30.

Lehman AF. Quality of life interview for the chronically mentally ill. *Eval Program Planning* 1988;11:51–62.

Liddle PF. The symptoms of chronic schizophrenia: a re-examination of the positive–negative dichotomy. *Br J Psychiatry* 1987;151:145–51.

Oliver J. Development of a quality of life profile for use in community services for the mentally ill. *Soc Work Soc Sci Rev* 1993;3:53–60.

The ICD-10 Classification of Mental & Behavioural Disorders. Diagnostic Criteria for Research. Geneva: World Health Organization, 1993.

Wykes T, Sturt E. The measurement of social behaviour in psychiatric patients: an assessment of the reliability and validity of the SBS schedule. *Br J Psychiatry* 1986;148:1–11.

Knowledge about how schizophrenia is distributed within and between cultures is an important indicator of possible theories of causation, as well as being important in planning mental health services. The development of agreed, reliable definitions of the diagnosis has been crucial to epidemiological research. The current state of knowledge is described here.

How common?

The incidence of schizophrenia is the number of new cases appearing, either expressed annually or as lifetime risk. The prevalence of schizophrenia is the number of cases at any one time point. These figures depend on whether ICD-10 or DSM-IV (or the previous, similar DSM-III-R) criteria are used. Because of the 6-month, rather than 1-month, criterion in DSM, the incidence and prevalence will be lower with DSM-IV than with ICD-10. Large, community-based surveys of geographically defined areas give prevalence estimates of between 0.2% and 0.7%. Incidence studies of epidemiological samples show that there will be about 2 new cases of ICD schizophrenia, or about 1 new case of DSM schizophrenia, per 10 000 population each year.

How global?

Schizophrenia exists in all cultures in all countries. The symptoms are surprisingly similar around the globe. Using clinical raters reliably trained to use the same diagnostic criteria, the World Health Organization showed, in two large field studies in 12 centers in 10 different developed and developing countries, that narrowly defined schizophrenia had similar incidence in all countries. However, there are some important differences. Although narrowly defined schizophrenia was recorded at roughly similar rates, broadly defined schizophrenia was found to differ in prevalence between countries. Secondly, the outcome of the illness was significantly better in developing than in developed countries. Why this should be is unknown. Possible explanations include different mixtures of etiologic factors, or differences in factors known to aid recovery, such as family support or decreased environmental stimulation.

Localities where apparently increased rates of schizophrenia have been described are shown in Figure 3.1. These are often due to migrational effects or genetic isolates.

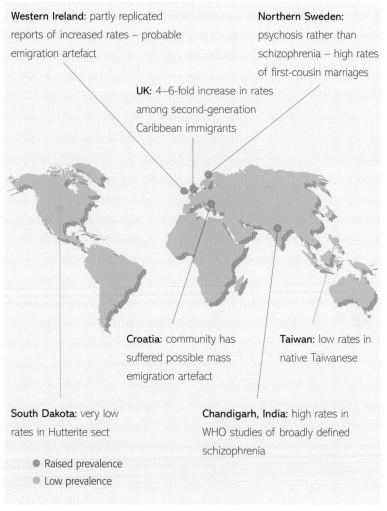

Western Ireland: partly replicated reports of increased rates – probable emigration artefact

Northern Sweden: psychosis rather than schizophrenia – high rates of first-cousin marriages

UK: 4–6-fold increase in rates among second-generation Caribbean immigrants

Croatia: community has suffered possible mass emigration artefact

Taiwan: low rates in native Taiwanese

South Dakota: very low rates in Hutterite sect

Chandigarh, India: high rates in WHO studies of broadly defined schizophrenia

● Raised prevalence
● Low prevalence

Figure 3.1 Reported pockets of increased and decreased schizophrenia around the world.

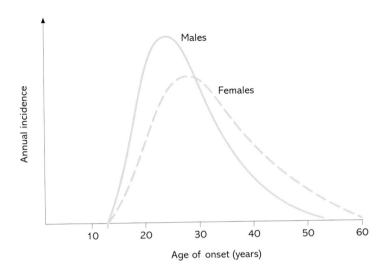

Figure 3.2 Annual incidence rates by gender.

Age and gender effects

The incidence of schizophrenia is roughly the same in men and women. Men, however, are slightly more likely to develop enduring negative symptoms than women, who have greater representation in the good prognosis group. Therefore, the prevalence of schizophrenia when defined in DSM-IV is higher in men. This difference is less pronounced in ICD-10. The peak age of onset in males is from 21 to 26 years, whereas in females the peak age of onset is from 25 to 32 years (Figure 3.2).

City life and schizophrenia

It has long been known that rates of schizophrenia are higher in urban than in rural areas. Early surveys seemed to show that this was due to the drift of people into urban areas after the illness started, rather than to higher rates of new cases in cities. However, recent large studies have confirmed that new cases arise more commonly in cities, with the rates being proportional to the degree of urbanization. This appears to be an unexpectedly large effect. The relative risk for large-city dwellers compared with rural residents is only 2–3-fold (Table 5.2) but, because much of the population lives in cities, the proportion of schizophrenia that can be explained on the basis of this factor is about one third. The factors associated with city life that contribute to the increased rate of schizophrenia remain to be clarified.

Course and outcome

The best outcome studies are those that prospectively follow up a cohort of consecutive first-episode patients, ideally from a defined catchment area, for at least 5 years. However, such studies are rare. Summarizing the best long-term studies available, there is a consensus that 15–20% of patients will make a complete recovery without relapse. At the other extreme, about 15% will effectively never recover from their first episode, remaining symptomatic and needing long-term, high levels of social and medical input. Between these two poles, most patients will recover at least partly from their first episode, but will not return to their premorbid level of functioning, or will suffer future relapses, or both (Figure 3.3). Suicide occurs in 5% of patients and is difficult to predict. Young men in the first 3 years of their illness are most at risk.

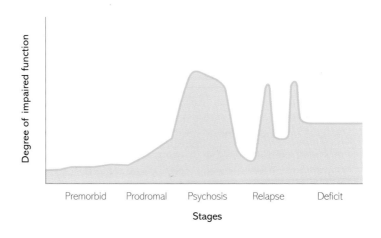

Figure 3.3 Profile of typical life course in schizophrenia.

Clues to long-term outcome can be gleaned from demographic factors and from the pattern of the first episode. Robust predictors of outcome are summarized in Table 3.1.

TABLE 3.1

Well-established predictors of outcome

Factor	Good outcome	Poor outcome
Demographic	Female	Male
	Married	Single
Genetic	Family history of affective disorder	Family history of schizophrenia
Onset	Good premorbid adjustment	Schizoid traits
	Acute onset	Slow onset
	Life event at onset	
	Early treatment	Long duration of untreated psychosis
Symptoms	Affective symptoms	Negative symptoms
		Obsessions
		Bizarre delusions
Psychosocial	Good response to treatment	High expressed emotion
		Substance misuse

Epidemiology – Key points

- The incidence of new cases of schizophrenia is 1–2 per 10 000 population per year.
- It exists in all countries and cultures, but prevalence rates vary.
- Onset is usually in early adult life; 20% will recover completely.
- Urban birth and living appear unexpectedly important in causing schizophrenia.

Key references

Castle D, Wessely S, Der G et al. The incidence of operationally defined schizophrenia in Camberwell 1965–84. *Br J Psychiatry* 1991;159:790–4.

Harrison G, Croudace T, Mason P et al. Predicting the long-term outcome of schizophrenia. *Psychol Med* 1996;26:697–705.

Hegarty JD, Baldessarini RJ, Tohen M et al. One hundred years of schizophrenia: a meta-analysis of the outcome literature. *Am J Psychiatry* 1994;151:1409–14.

Hopper K, Wanderling J. Revisiting the developed versus developing country distinction in course and outcome in schizophrenia. *Schizophr Bull* 2000;26:835–46.

Kendler KS, Gallagher TJ, Abelson JM, Kessler RC. Lifetime prevalence, demographic risk factors and diagnostic validity of nonaffective psychoses in a US community sample. The National Comorbidity Survey. *Arch Gen Psychiatry* 1996;53:1022–31.

Marcelis M, Takei N, van Os J. Urbanization and risk for schizophrenia. Does the effect operate before or around the time of illness onset? *Psychol Med* 1999;29:1197–1203.

Mortensen PB, Pedersen CB, Westergaard T et al. Effects of family history and place and season of birth on the risk of schizophrenia. *N Engl J Med* 1999;340:603–8.

Pedersen CB, Mortensen PB. Evidence of a dose–response relationship between urbanicity during upbringing and schizophrenia risk. *Arch Gen Psychiatry* 2001;58:1039–48.

Sartorius N, Jablesky A, Koorten A et al. Early manifestations and first-contact incidence of schizophrenia in different cultures. *Psychol Med* 1986;16:909–28.

Thara R, Eaton WW. Outcome of schizophrenia: the Madras longitudinal study. *Aust N Z J Psychiatry* 1996;30:516–22.

The biggest single clue we have about the cause of schizophrenia is that it often runs in families. Although this observation was made first in the opening years of the 20th century, until relatively recently it was disputed whether or not this family clustering was truly a genetic effect.

The classic studies

The most straightforward studies in population genetics are family studies. Usually, a series of schizophrenic individuals, known as probands or index cases, is selected and rates of schizophrenia are assessed in their biological families. These rates are compared with rates in the families of control probands, usually healthy volunteers. Studies include family history studies, which rely on the account of the proband and one or more other relatives to piece together the family tree, including an operational diagnosis on any relatives with an apparent psychiatric disorder. Other studies employ family interviews where all members are interviewed face-to-face. As expected, family interview studies are more reliable, but harder work. For severe disorders like schizophrenia, family history studies produce adequate results. To express the results as rates, the number of affected relatives is divided by the total number and age-corrected for relatives who are either too young to have the disorder or are not yet through the age range at highest risk.

The risk to relatives depends firstly on how close the relative is to the proband (Figure 4.1). Spouses are at slightly increased risk because of assortative mating (i.e. selection of similar partners). The diagnostic system used affects the risk to relatives, as it does prevalence, and fewer relatives will be diagnosed with DSM-IV schizophrenia than with ICD-10 schizophrenia. Recent studies have shown an unexpected effect of gender. Relatives of female probands have higher rates of schizophrenia than relatives of male probands.

Family studies can never give conclusive proof of genetic effects, as familiality could be due to a shared environmental factor. Nevertheless,

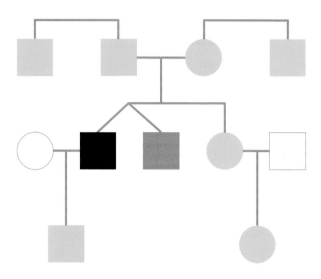

Figure 4.1 A genogram showing risk of schizophrenia in relatives. Proband (black); an identical twin (red) shares 100% of genes, risk 45%; a first-degree relative (blue) shares 50% of genes, risk 10%; a second-degree relative (yellow) shares 25% of genes, risk 3%.

family studies have shown that if there is a genetic effect, it does not follow a recognized Mendelian pattern of autosomal dominance, such as Huntington's disease, or recessiveness, such as cystic fibrosis.

Twin studies

Twin studies involve probands with schizophrenia who are either identical (monozygotic: MZ) or non-identical (dizygotic: DZ) twins. Concordance rates in the two types of twins are compared by looking at the rate at which co-twins also have schizophrenia. Monozygotic twins share 100% of their genes and dizygotic twins share about 50%. The consensus from population-based studies is that concordance rates are about 45% for MZ co-twins compared with 15% for DZ co-twins. The fact that concordance is less than 100% in MZ twins suggests that non-genetic, environmental factors also operate. The offspring of the unaffected MZ co-twins in discordant pairs, however, seem also to be at increased risk of schizophrenia, suggesting that the co-twins still carry a genetic predisposition for the disease.

Adoption studies offer the most watertight evidence for genetic effects, as family environment is taken out of the equation. There are two types of study: follow-up and follow-back. Follow-up adoption studies trace the biological children of schizophrenic mothers, who were adopted into normal families at birth, and compare the number of offspring that develop schizophrenia with control adoptees of healthy mothers. Follow-back studies start with a group of schizophrenic adults who were known to be adopted at birth. The biological parents are traced and their rates of illness compared with those in the biological parents of control adoptees. Both methods have shown that it is biological parentage rather than adoptive parentage that predisposes to schizophrenia.

The extended phenotype

The results from family, twin and adoption studies subjected to modern diagnostic criteria support the notion that a proportion of biological relatives of schizophrenic probands, while not having frank schizophrenia, have an unusual cluster of traits. This was previously called latent schizophrenia, but is now termed schizotypal personality disorder. A number of other schizophrenia spectrum disorders are found in the families of schizophrenic probands (Table 4.1).

Measurements of cognitive abnormalities provide an alternative approach for defining the phenotype. Impairments in attention, evoked potentials such as the P50 wave, working memory, and smooth-pursuit and saccadic eye movements are often seen in patients and their families. These cognitive abnormalities may be more sensitive than diagnostic categories for indicating the presence of genes for schizophrenia. They can supplement the use of diagnostic categories in genetic studies, enhancing the likelihood of detecting these genes.

What is the pattern of inheritance?

It is clear that schizophrenia is not transmitted in a Mendelian fashion. It conforms to the pattern of other 'complex' disorders, such as ischemic heart disease. Any model, however, must explain why

TABLE 4.1

Disorders found at increased rates in families of schizophrenic probands

- Schizophrenia
- Schizoaffective disorder
- Delusional disorder
- Schizotypal disorder
- Atypical psychosis
- Major depression

schizophrenia is so common, with a lifetime prevalence approaching 1% (i.e. 20 times more common than the most common Mendelian disorder, cystic fibrosis). It must also explain why schizophrenia persists in the population when it is accompanied by obvious biological disadvantage. Possible models are outlined in Table 4.2.

The genome

Clinically, schizophrenia varies widely in its symptoms and course. This has often been taken as evidence for etiologic heterogeneity, either with several different mutations giving slightly different clinical pictures, or with familial and non-familial forms. However, several mechanisms that may alter the extent to which a gene is expressed are now known. Partial penetrance or variable expressivity can occur so that the same gene can produce a range of effects, such as in neurofibromatosis where the gene that produces an 'elephant man' effect in one person will produce only a few skin speckles in another. Interaction between genes (epistasis) also occurs.

The size and power of studies performed indicates that there is unlikely to be any single gene that confers a relative risk of schizophrenia greater than threefold. Quantitative genetic studies have ruled out the explanation that it is a collection of single-gene disorders. The current picture is of a polygenic disorder with environmental factors acting on the penetrance of several susceptibility genes.

TABLE 4.2

Possible genetic mechanisms in schizophrenia

Model	Mechanism	Comment
Polygenic–multifactorial	Many small genes plus many small environmental factors	Difficult to prove
Oligogenic	A few genes (4 or 5) interacting with each other and with environmental effects	Currently has the most support
Genetic heterogeneity	Different forms of schizophrenia, each the result of a major gene effect	This occurs in Alzheimer's disease. Might expect to find identifiable subtypes that breed true
Causal heterogeneity	High proportion of non-genetic phenocopies	But genes probably explain 70–80% of schizophrenia
High rates of new mutations	New mutations in paternal germ line	Would explain why schizophrenia persists despite disadvantages

The search for genes in schizophrenia is difficult for several reasons (Table 4.3). The approach known as linkage analysis focuses either on multiply affected pedigrees apparently involving major genes, or on analysis of large samples of sibling pairs discordant for the disorder, so-called association studies. The second approach is better for genes of small effect and where the mode of inheritance is unclear. Known genetic markers throughout the genome (polymorphisms) are then used to locate the faulty gene, a technique known as positional cloning. Significant linkage has been reported in more than one study to regions on chromosomes 1q, 5q, 8p, 13q, 18p and 22q, supporting the notion that there are several vulnerability genes. The rare, neurodevelopmental velocardiofacial syndrome (VCFS) results from a gene deletion on 22q. Schizophrenia develops in 30% of VCFS patients. The search can be

TABLE 4.3

Difficulties in the search for a gene in schizophrenia

- The limits of the phenotype are not well understood (e.g. should schizotypes be included?)
- The mode of inheritance is unclear. This is important for linkage analysis, but less so for association studies
- The incidence of phenocopies (non-genetic schizophrenia) is unknown, but needs to be specified for linkage analysis
- It is unclear which genes or chromosomes are candidates for linkage
- It is not known whether the results from studies of highly familial schizophrenia are applicable to all schizophrenia
- Genes probably have small individual effect, so large samples are needed

helped by finding candidate genes that code for proteins that plausibly play a part in schizophrenia, such as those that code for neurotransmitters or their receptors. The dopamine and serotonin systems have been examined in this way, and polymorphisms of the genes for the D_3 and $5HT_{2a}$ receptors have been shown to be associated with schizophrenia by some groups. Such genes are likely to be important in other aspects of the disorder, such as drug treatment response.

Genetics – Key points

- Having a close relative with schizophrenia increases one's own risk 15-fold.
- Identical twins show a 45% concordance rate.
- Individual vulnerability genes exist.
- Genes are each of small effect and act additively.

Key references

Burnet P, Eastwood SL, Harrison PJ. 5HT$_{1a}$ and 5HT$_{2a}$ receptor mRNAs and binding sites are differentially affected in schizophrenia. *Neuropsychopharmacology* 1996; 15:422–35.

Cardno A, Marshall EJ, McDonald A et al. Heritability estimates for psychotic disorders: the Maudsley twin psychosis study. *Arch Gen Psychiatry* 1999;56:162–7.

Cardno AG, Murphy KC, Jones CA et al. Expanded CAG/CTG repeats in schizophrenia. A study of clinical correlates. *Br J Psychiatry* 1996;169: 766–71.

Freedman R, Coon H, Myles-Worsley M et al. Linkage of a neurophysiological deficit in schizophrenia to a chromosome 15 locus. *Proc Natl Acad Sci USA* 1997;94:587–92.

Gurling HMD, Kalsi G, Brynjolfson J et al. Genomewide genetic linkage analysis confirms the presence of susceptibility loci for schizophrenia. *Am J Hum Genet* 2001;68: 661–73.

Kendler KS, Gruenberg AM. An independent analysis of the Danish adoption study of schizophrenia VI. The patterns of psychiatric illness as defined by DSM III in adoptees and relatives. *Arch Gen Psychiatry* 1984;41:555–64.

Kendler KS, MacLean CJ, O'Neill FA et al. Evidence for a schizophrenia vulnerability locus on chromosome 8p in the Irish study of high-density families. *Am J Psychiatry* 1996;153: 1534–40.

Nimgaonkar VL, Sanders AR, Ganguli R et al. Association study of schizophrenia and the dopamine D3 receptor gene locus in two independent samples. *Am J Hum Genet* 1996;67:505–14.

Williams J, Spurlock G, McGuffin P et al. Association between schizophrenia and T102C polymorphism of the 5HT$_{2a}$ receptor gene. *Lancet* 1996;347:1294–6.

Wright P, Donaldson PT, Underhill JA et al. Genetic association of the HLA DRB1 locus on chromosome 6p21.3 with schizophrenia. *Am J Psychiatry* 1996;153:1530–3.

5 Neurodevelopmental theories and environmental factors

Until the mid 1980s, schizophrenia was believed to be an essentially degenerative disorder. Its natural history, with onset in early adulthood, progressive cognitive and functional impairments, and the findings of apparent cerebral atrophy in the first brain-imaging studies seemed to support this notion. However, the range of findings outlined in Table 5.1 suggested that the brain changes pre-dated the onset of the disorder and perhaps were sequelae of much earlier environmental insults or genetic processes occurring during brain development. It was suggested that a static lesion, either genetically or environmentally mediated during brain development, expresses its effects as a function of the maturational stage of the brain; in the case of schizophrenia, the characteristic symptoms emerge only during the final stages of brain development in adolescence. The finding, in about 5% of young patients, of a variety of clinically unsuspected neurodevelopmental lesions on computed tomography (CT) or magnetic resonance imaging (MRI) supports this view (Figure 5.1).

TABLE 5.1

Evidence for schizophrenia being a neurodevelopmental disorder

- Non-progressive structural brain abnormalities early in the illness
- Increased rate of major neurodevelopmental brain lesions
- Association with obstetric complications, leading to earlier age at onset
- Unusual developmental trajectory in childhood with cognitive and behavioral impairments
- Increased rate of minor physical anomalies
- Histological and morphological abnormalities at autopsy
- Association with known neurodevelopmental genetic disorders (e.g. velocardiofacial syndrome)

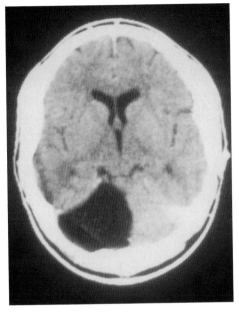

Figure 5.1 Computed tomography brain scan showing a clinically unsuspected neuro-developmental cyst in a neurologically normal 22-year-old schizophrenic man.

Neurodevelopmental risk factors

Non-genetic factors probably account for about 30% of the risk for schizophrenia. Some established risk factors act early in life (Table 5.2). Obstetric complications generally appear to increase the risk of schizophrenia. During pregnancy, risk factors include rubella, and probably influenza, infections in the first or second trimester and antepartum bleeding. At birth, asphyxia and low birthweight, especially with intrauterine growth retardation, are risk factors, as are certain brain insults and infections in childhood.

Early developmental delays

Longitudinal follow-up studies of large birth cohorts have shown that the 1–2% of the sample who go on to develop adult schizophrenia show slight delays in motor, speech and intellectual milestones compared with the rest of the cohort. These differences are subtle, such as walking delayed by 1–2 months. Certain problems, such as developmental receptive language disorders, are particularly linked to later schizophrenia.

TABLE 5.2

Known early environmental risk factors for schizophrenia

Risk factor	Probable increase in risk
Intrauterine infections	1.2
Unwanted pregnancy	4
Rhesus incompatibility	2
Antenatal starvation	2
Birth complications	4
Winter birth	1.1
Childhood head injury	1.2
Childhood encephalitis	7
Raised in city	2.4

Secondary schizophrenias

The so-called secondary schizophrenias fit less easily into the neurodevelopmental formulation. The psychotic symptoms in these cases appear to be caused by a primary, organic disorder: either a known physical disorder or a clinically unsuspected brain lesion. Table 5.3 lists those medical disorders in which a clear or possible association with schizophrenia-like disorders has been reported. Clinically recommended screening investigations are outlined in Table 5.4.

Psychosocial risk factors

There is emerging evidence again for the role of non-biological risk factors in schizophrenia. Street drug use has long been known to be an important trigger of relapse, but was thought not to play a truly causal role in illness onset. New research suggests that cannabis use in adolescence increases the risk of schizophrenia 2–3 fold. Psychosocial explanations for the high rates of psychosis seen in black Caribbeans in the UK and other European countries also appear likely, because the size of the effect has been shown to depend on the cultural milieu, with rates highest for black Caribbeans living in mainly white areas.

TABLE 5.3

Physical diseases with an increased risk of schizophrenic symptoms

- Epilepsy, temporal lobe
- Infections:
  - limbic encephalitis; subacute sclerosing panencephalitis
  - neurosyphilis
  - neurocysticercosis
  - HIV disease
- Cerebral trauma
- Cerebrovascular disease (late-onset schizophrenia)
- Demyelinating diseases:
  - multiple sclerosis (with temporal plaques)
  - Schilder's disease
  - metachromatic leukodystrophy
- Neurodevelopmental disorders
  - velocardiofacial syndrome

TABLE 5.4

Screening investigations in first-episode schizophrenia

First-line	Second-line
• Neurological examination	• CT/MRI scan
• Complete blood cell count	• Autoantibodies
• Routine blood biochemistry	• Serum calcium
• Thyroid function	• Syphilis serology
• Liver function	• HIV serology
• Electroencephalogram	• Chromosome studies
• Drug screen: urine or hair	• Serum copper
	• Arylsulfatase-A
	• CSF examination

Neurodevelopmental theories and environmental factors – Key points

- Early neurodevelopmental, non-genetic risk factors exist for schizophrenia.
- Birth complications increase the child's risk of schizophrenia in later life 4-fold.
- Psychosocial risk factors are re-emerging in research.
- Street drug use appears to increase risk of schizophrenia as well as relapse.

Key references

Brown AS, Susser E, Cohen SG. Schizophrenia following prenatal rubella exposure: gestational timing and diagnostic specificity. *Schizophrenia Res* 1998;29:17–18.

Cannon M, Caspi A, Moffitt TE et al. Evidence or early childhood, pandevelopmental impairment specific to schizophreniform disorder. *Arch Gen Psychiatry* 2002;59:449–56.

Hollister JM, Laing P, Mednick SA. Rhesus incompatibility as a risk factor for schizophrenia in male adults. *Arch Gen Psychiatry* 1996;53:19–24.

Howlin P, Mawhood L, Rutter M. Autism and developmental receptive language disorder – a follow up comparison in early adult life 2: social, behavioural and psychiatric outcomes. *J Child Psychol Psychiatry* 2000;41:561–78.

Hultman CM, Ohman A, Cnattingius S et al. Prenatal and neonatal risk factors for schizophrenia. *Br J Psychiatry* 1997;170:128–33.

Jones P, Rodgers B, Murray R, Marmot M. Child developmental risk factors for adult schizophrenia in the British 1946 birth cohort. *Lancet* 1994;344:1398–402.

Murray RM, Lewis SW, Reveley AM. Towards an aetiological classification of schizophrenia. *Lancet* 1985;i:1023–6.

Rantakallio P, Jones P, Moring J, von Wendt L. Association between central nervous system infections during childhood and adult-onset schizophrenia and other psychoses: a 28 year follow up. *Int J Epidemiol* 1997;26:837–43.

Weinberger DR. Implications of normal brain development for the pathogenesis of schizophrenia. *Arch Gen Psychiatry* 1987;44:660–9.

Our knowledge of the neuroanatomy of schizophrenia is derived from four major sources:

- structural imaging
- neuropsychology and functional imaging
- psychopharmacology
- postmortem neurochemical and structural investigations.

Of these procedures, structural imaging has been used most extensively to examine the brains of patients with schizophrenia.

Pneumoencephalography

The first structural imaging studies were performed using pneumo-encephalography (PEG), a technique based on the x-ray contrast in air injected into the lumbar subarachnoid space, bone and brain tissue. PEG studies documented a number of abnormalities in patients with schizophrenia, including enlargement of the ventricular system, a fluid-filled system in the interior of the brain that serves as a natural shock absorber. However, the invasive nature of the procedure limited its application and eventually led to the abandonment of its use.

CT scanning

The next major development in structural imaging was the introduction of CT scanning, an in-vivo x-ray-based imaging technique for visualizing the brain (e.g. Figure 5.1). The advent of CT scanning enabled investigators to examine, in a relatively safe manner for the first time, brain structure in large groups of patients with schizophrenia. Eve Johnstone and colleagues conducted the first CT study in schizophrenia and confirmed the observation of ventricular enlargement. This finding has been reproduced many times and represents one of the most commonly observed biological findings in schizophrenia.

The other major abnormality revealed by CT scanning is a widening of the cortical sulci, which separate the different cerebral gyri. These observations have greatly influenced our understanding of schizophrenia pathophysiology. They provided strong evidence that a significant proportion of patients with schizophrenia are characterized by structural abnormalities of the brain. In addition, they helped to reawaken interest in schizophrenia as a brain disease and counteracted the prevailing view at that time of schizophrenia being caused by psychosocial factors.

Limitations of CT. There are, however, two major limitations to CT scanning. First, CT scans do not permit sufficient resolution of cortical and subcortical gray matter (i.e. nerve cells) and white matter (i.e. fibre tracts connecting different nerve cells). The lack of resolution precludes the morphological assessment of specific cortical and subcortical structures. Second, although ventricular enlargement and cortical sulcal widening suggest that patients with schizophrenia may have relatively less brain tissue than normal controls, they are non-specific measures and cannot tell us where in the brain the tissue loss occurs, or whether the decrease in tissue is due to a failure to develop or to neurodegenerative processes. There are a number of structures anatomically related to the ventricular system, including basal ganglia nuclei, limbic system structures (i.e. the amygdala and hippocampus), thalamus, and cortical white matter. Ventricular enlargement could be secondary to morphological abnormalities in any one or combination of these structures. Similarly, sulcal widening could be secondary to changes in cortical gray and/or white matter. Only the direct measurement of these two cortical tissue types would allow the cause of sulcal widening to be determined.

MRI

The advent of MRI enabled investigators to overcome the limitations of CT scanning. MRI produces high-quality images, based on the use of magnetic energy and the water content of different tissue types. MRI images can be segmented into the three different tissue types or compartments:

- gray matter, both cortical and subcortical
- white matter
- cerebrospinal fluid (CSF).

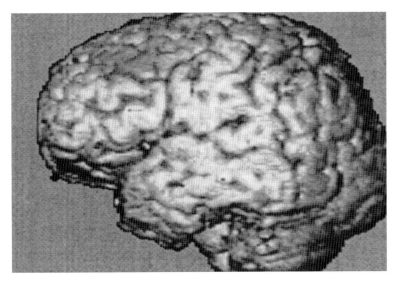

Figure 6.1 A three-dimensional representation of the brain constructed from magnetic resonance imaging.

These three compartments can each be measured, and for the first time investigators could examine whether patients with schizophrenia were characterized by specific brain morphological abnormalities. MRI images can also be obtained in a three-dimensional format, from which three-dimensional representations of the brain can be constructed (Figure 6.1). These three-dimensional representations facilitate the morphological assessment of specific cortical gyri (Figure 6.2).

MRI studies were able to confirm the previous findings of enlarged ventricles, with patients exhibiting about a one-third increase in ventricular volume compared with controls (Figure 6.3), and increased sulcal widening (Figure 6.4). MRI studies demonstrated for the first time the involvement of cortical and subcortical gray matter structures. Specifically, patients with schizophrenia were shown to exhibit decreased volume of the neocortex, by about 5%, with specific gray matter reductions in the prefrontal, superior temporal and inferior parietal heteromodal cortices. These brain regions are the neuroanatomical substrate for the complex cognitive behaviors that are uniquely affected in patients with schizophrenia. In addition to volume reductions in these areas, several studies have found that patients with

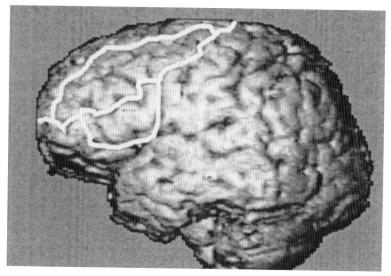

Figure 6.2 A three-dimensional representation of the brain with sulcal landmarks for the inferior and middle prefrontal gyri demarcated.

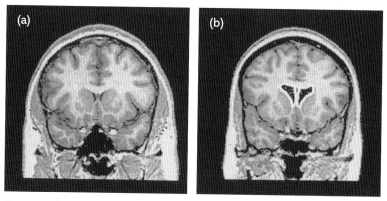

Figure 6.3 Patients with schizophrenia commonly have enlarged ventricles: (a) normal control; (b) patient with schizophrenia, on MRI in coronal plane.

schizophrenia have a reversal or loss of the normal asymmetry of these structures.

MRI studies have also documented decreased volume of limbic system structures such as the amygdala, hippocampus and parahippocampus (see Figure 6.5). These structures are involved in the regulation of emotions and various forms of memory. The

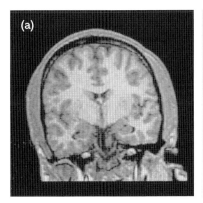
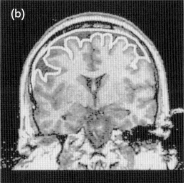

Figure 6.4 Patients with schizophrenia have increased sulcal widening, which is associated with increased cortical cerebrospinal fluid (shown in the highlighted areas): (a) normal control; (b) patient with schizophrenia, on MRI.

magnitude of these changes is relatively small (Table 6.1), but the observations have been shown to be highly reliable, especially for the hippocampus. Finally, MRI studies have documented a decrease in the volume of specific thalamic nuclei and in the total volume of the thalamus. Thalamic nuclei play a central role in gating the flow of information to the cerebral cortex and in regulating the activation of specific cortical brain areas in response to external or internal stimuli or signals. These MRI results are consistent with postmortem study

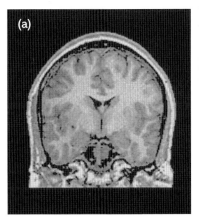
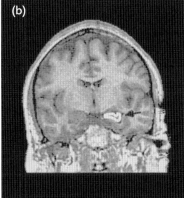

Figure 6.5 Patients with schizophrenia often have a hippocampus of abnormal shape or volume (see arrow): (a) normal control; (b) patient with schizophrenia.

TABLE 6.1

How big are the changes in brain structure in schizophrenia?

Total ventricular volume	Increased	30%
Total cerebral cortical volume	Decreased	2–4%
Heteromodal association cortex (e.g. STG)	Decreased	5–10%
Medial temporal lobe (e.g. hippocampus)	Decreased	5–10%
Thalamus	Decreased	10–40%

STG, superior temporal gyrus

reports that have documented decreased volume of the medial dorsal and pulvinar thalamic nuclei.

In addition to locating the areas of the brain affected by schizophrenia, MRI studies have also been useful for studying:

- pathophysiological models of schizophrenia
- neuroanatomy of schizophrenia symptoms
- morphological consequences of exposure to environmental risk factors
- etiologic theories of schizophrenia.

For example, longitudinal studies with serial MRI evaluations have been used to address the question of whether schizophrenia is a neurodevelopmental disorder, with fixed morphological abnormalities, or a neurodegenerative disorder, with progressive changes in brain structure. There are relatively few longitudinal studies, but they suggest that a subgroup of patients may exhibit progressive changes in brain structure over the course of their illness (Table 6.2). These changes have been observed in both cortical and ventricular structures.

MRI studies have also documented gender differences. Male patients with schizophrenia have been found in some, but not all, studies to have greater reductions in tissue volume, particularly in the temporal lobes. These morphological differences may represent the interaction of the disease process of schizophrenia with normal gender differences in brain development and structure, and may provide a structural

TABLE 6.2

Evidence for progressive brain changes in schizophrenia

- Increasing functional disability
- Increasingly refractory symptoms
- Structural brain abnormalities correlate with length of illness
- Structural brain abnormalities progress in early-onset schizophrenia
- Progressive neurocognitive deficits

explanation for the observation that the course of schizophrenia is frequently more benign in female than in male patients.

Several studies have observed a relationship between decreased volume of the superior temporal gyral gray matter and hallucinations and delusions or positive formal thought disorder. Hallucinations and delusions are more frequently associated with decreased volume of the anterior superior temporal gyrus, and positive formal thought disorder is more frequently associated with decreased volume of the posterior superior temporal gyrus.

MRI has also been used to show that patients with schizophrenia have a loss of the normal asymmetry of the cerebral hemispheres, especially of the planum temporale, a region of the brain involved in audition and language. These observations have led to the development of etiologic hypotheses concerning abnormalities in the normal process of brain lateralization.

Brain pathology

The reduced cerebral cortex thickness observed with MRI appears to result from a loss of the supportive glial cells, such as astrocytes, leading to an increased packing of neurons (Table 6.3). Glial cells, particularly astrocytes, promote synaptic function. Reduced synaptic and dendritic complexity is seen. These changes might result from early developmental abnormalities, from an increase in the synaptic pruning that normally occurs in adolescence, or from a later, progressive process. Long-term antipsychotic drug administration has also been shown to increase glial density.

TABLE 6.3

Histopathological findings in cerebral cortex in schizophrenia

- Reduced glial cell density
- Increased neuronal density
- Aberrant migration of neurons
- Smaller neurons
- Loss of synapses
- Loss of dendritic complexity

Future directions

The observation of multiple cortical and subcortical gray matter morphological abnormalities raises the question of whether there is a disturbance in the white matter fiber tracts that connect these regions. There have been previous reports of decreased white matter volume, but such changes have not been observed consistently. Moreover, traditional MRI structural images are not able to differentiate specific

---

Neuroanatomy and structural imaging – Key points

- Patients with schizophrenia exhibit gray matter reductions in the prefrontal, superior temporal and inferior parietal heteromodal cortices.
- Patients with schizophrenia have decreased volume of subcortical structures, including the amygdala, hippocampus, parahippocampus and thalamus.
- A subgroup of patients may exhibit progressive changes in brain structure over the course of their illness.
- Male patients with schizophrenia have been found to have greater volume reductions in the temporal lobes.
- Hallucinations, delusions and positive formal thought disorder are associated with decreased volume of the superior temporal gyrus.

fiber tracts. The development of diffusion tensor imaging (DTI) allows for the evaluation of the integrity of specific fiber tracts. Initial DTI studies suggest that patients with schizophrenia may have a general disruption in the organization of the major fiber tracts, perhaps particularly in those tracts linking frontal and temporal cortex. Whether these white matter changes precede or result from cortical changes is not clear. Future studies with more refined analytic techniques will allow for more detailed investigations of these tracts.

Key references

Andreasen NC, Arndt S, Swayze II V et al. Thalamic abnormalities in schizophrenia visualized through magnetic resonance image averaging. *Science* 1994;266:294.

Barta PE, Pearlson GD, Brill 2nd LB et al. Planum temporale asymmetry reversal in schizophrenia: replication and relationship to gray matter abnormalities. *Am J Psychiatry* 1997;154:661–7.

Bryant NL, Buchanan RW, Vladar K et al. Gender differences in temporal lobe structures of patients with schizophrenia: a volumetric MRI study. *Am J Psychiatry* 1999;156: 603–9.

Buchanan RW, Breier A, Kirkpatrick B et al. Structural abnormalities in deficit and nondeficit schizophrenia. *Am J Psychiatry* 1993;150:59–65.

Buchanan RW, Vladar K, Barta PE, Pearlson GD. A structural evaluation of the prefrontal cortex in schizophrenia. *Am J Psychiatry* 1998;155:1049–55.

Frederikse M, Lu A, Aylward E et al. Sex differences in inferior parietal lobule volume in schizophrenia. *Am J Psychiatry* 2000;157:422–7.

Johnstone EC, Crow TJ, Frith DC et al. Cerebral ventricular size and cognitive impairment in schizophrenia. *Lancet* 1976;ii:970.

Lim KO, Hedehus M, Moseley M et al. Compromised white matter tract integrity in schizophrenia inferred from diffusion tensor imaging. *Arch Gen Psychiatry* 1999;56:367–74.

Mathalon DH, Sullivan EV, Lim KO, Pfefferbaum A. Progressive brain volume changes and the clinical course of schizophrenia in men: a longitudinal magnetic resonance imaging study. *Arch Gen Psychiatry* 2001;58:148–57.

Pearlson GD, Petty RG, Ross CA, Tien AY. Schizophrenia: a disease of heteromodal association cortex? *Neuropsychopharmacology* 1996;14:1–17.

Shenton ME, Kikinis R, Jolesz FA et al. Abnormalities of the left temporal lobe and thought disorder in schizophrenia: a quantitative magnetic resonance imaging study. *N Engl J Med* 1992;327:604–12.

Wright IC, Rabe-Hesketh S, Woodruff PW et al. Meta-analysis of regional brain volumes in schizophrenia. *Am J Psychiatry* 2000;157:16–25.

Zipursky RB, Lim KO, Sullivan EV et al. Widespread cerebral gray matter volume deficits in schizophrenia. *Arch Gen Psychiatry* 1992;49:195–205.

The original name for schizophrenia, dementia praecox, reflects the appreciation of even the earliest investigators of the primary role of neurocognitive impairments in schizophrenia. However, the precise nature and extent of these impairments remains unknown. Are there specific, fundamental impairments that all patients share and that are responsible for the broad range of neurocognitive abnormalities observed in schizophrenia, or do the multiple abnormalities reflect the widespread pathophysiological involvement of the brain? When do neurocognitive impairments first become manifest, and under what circumstances do they progress? What is the relationship of neurocognitive impairments to other aspects of schizophrenia?

What is the nature of neurocognitive impairments in patients with schizophrenia?

Patients with schizophrenia present with a broad range of neurocognitive impairments (see Table 7.1). Many of these impairments may be detected through the use of neuropsychological assessments

TABLE 7.1

Severest cognitive deficits in schizophrenia

Deficit	Functions impaired	Tests of impairment
Attention	Vigilance	Continuous performance task
	Visual search	Span of apprehension task
Memory	Episodic memory (recalling events)	Paired associate learning
	Working (short-term) memory	Delayed response tasks
Executive function	Problem solving; mental set shifting	Wisconsin Card Sort
	Inhibiting habitual responses	Stroop task

and include abnormalities in: attention; executive functions, including problem solving; verbal and visual memory; working memory; verbal fluency; and processing speed. In contrast, primary and secondary sensory functions have been traditionally considered to be relatively intact. However, there is emerging evidence to suggest that patients with schizophrenia may exhibit subtle impairments in early sensory information processing, which may contribute to their impaired performance on more complex neuropsychological tasks.

In addition to impaired performance on neuropsychological assessments, patients with schizophrenia also exhibit other types of cognitive abnormalities. These types of abnormalities are usually only detected using sophisticated computerized assessment techniques, and include impairments in eye-tracking and sensory gating. There are two major types of eye-tracking abnormalities. One type involves the smooth-pursuit eye movement system and is reflected in an inability to track moving objects normally. The other type involves the saccadic eye movement system. Patients with schizophrenia are less able to inhibit inappropriate saccadic eye movement intrusions into their smooth-pursuit eye movements, and they are less able to produce saccadic eye movements in the direction opposite to a visual stimulus.

The other prominent cognitive impairment that patients with schizophrenia frequently exhibit is an inability to suppress their response to repetitive sensory stimuli. Normal individuals are able to gradually ignore repetitive stimuli, whereas patients with schizophrenia experience each stimulus as a novel stimulus. This abnormality is thought to be related to the heightened distractibility that afflicts patients with schizophrenia. The P50 evoked-potential paradigm is used to detect the presence of this abnormality.

Family and twin studies suggest that several of these neurocognitive impairments may not only be characteristic features of schizophrenia, but may also be present in non-affected family members. In particular, abnormalities of attention, verbal memory, eye-tracking and P50 have been shown to occur at a higher than expected rate in family members than in the general population. These observations have led to the supposition that these impairments may represent alternative phenotypic markers of the illness (see Chapter 4).

Neurocognitive impairments: when do they occur?

The results of high-risk and large-scale birth cohort studies and studies of military inductees who have gone on to develop schizophrenia provide compelling evidence that patients with schizophrenia exhibit subtle neurocognitive impairments prior to the onset of more florid psychotic symptoms. These impairments may be present in early childhood and are already present in the first episode (Table 7.2). For example, retrospective studies of IQ test scores performed routinely during childhood show that those children who will later develop schizophrenia have slightly, but significantly, lower mean scores than do either age- and social-class-matched normal children, or siblings. The most convincing studies have been those of large, unselected birth cohorts followed up and tested at regular intervals. At the time of onset of positive psychotic symptoms, there is usually a further decline in cognitive function. Patients will typically exhibit a 5–10 point decline in their IQ.

TABLE 7.2

Neurocognitive deficits present in the first episode

- Spatial working memory
- Recognition memory
- Planning
- Attentional set shifting, causing perseveration
- Smell identification

What is the pathophysiology of neurocognitive impairments?

Neurocognitive impairments may reflect the involvement of specific brain regions or neural circuits or they may reflect a more global involvement of the brain. There is evidence for both hypotheses. The pattern of predominant impairments suggests the relatively selective involvement of frontotemporal areas. The results of functional imaging studies are also consistent with the selective involvement of frontotemporal areas, though this may be due in part to the nature of cognitive tasks studied. These studies also implicate the hippocampus in the pathophysiology of these impairments. On the other hand, patients with schizophrenia exhibit a broad range of neurocognitive impairments, and there is emerging evidence that patients exhibit abnormalities in the initial processing of sensory information, as well as more complex impairments. These latter findings are consistent with a more global involvement of the brain.

What is the relationship of neurocognitive impairments to other aspects of schizophrenia?

The relationship between cognitive impairments and individual symptom clusters and other domains of schizophrenia psychopathology has been the focus of extensive investigation. Patients with negative symptoms and symptoms of behavioral disorganization are more likely to exhibit clinically significant neurocognitive impairments than patients without these symptoms. Several studies have suggested that negative symptoms are selectively associated with impaired performance on neuropsychological measures sensitive to lesions of the frontal or parietal lobes. Patients with negative symptoms have also been shown to be the most impaired on tasks requiring self-generated, rather than stimulus-driven, activity. In contrast, disorganized patients are characterized by impaired performance on measures of distractibility, and they are also more likely to show an inability to inhibit inappropriate behavioral responses.

Patients with schizophrenia are characterized by poor social and occupational functioning. There has been a growing appreciation of the central role that neurocognitive impairments play in the development of these functional disabilities. Impairments of verbal memory, language, vigilance and executive function have been shown to be determinants of poor social and community function. Impairments of memory and executive and processing speed have been related to poor occupational outcome.

The relationship of neurocognitive impairments to the broad range of symptom and functional outcomes suggests that the development of effective treatments for these impairments would have far-ranging beneficial effects on patients with schizophrenia.

Functional imaging

Whatever else underlies the symptoms and deficits of schizophrenia, there is plainly a disturbance of brain function. Schizophrenia research has, therefore, been quick to use imaging techniques that demonstrate disturbances in brain function. However, it was not until the late 1970s that neuroscientists came to believe that, just as in other tissues (e.g. muscle), the blood flow and metabolism of brain tissue increased when a region was specifically active. The invention of imaging techniques that are able to show regional cerebral blood flow or metabolism confirmed that the blood flow to regions of primary motor or sensory cortex increases by 5–10% a few seconds after movement or perception begins. Similar changes of lesser magnitude also occur in brain regions executing a complex cognitive task, such as solving a puzzle. These changes can be used to clarify which areas of the brain are being used to do specific tasks.

PET, SPET, BOLD and MRS. The main functional imaging techniques are outlined in Table 7.3. Positron emission tomography (PET) and single-photon emission tomography (SPET) were the first true functional brain-scanning techniques. They both rely on intravenous injection or inhalation of radioactive tracers, which are taken up into the brain in proportion to local blood flow and produce a map of glucose metabolism or regional cerebral blood flow (rCBF). PET uses radioactive isotopes with short half-lives, which limits the amount of radiation received and enables repeated measurements in one session. PET isotopes decay to release two gamma rays, or photons, whereas SPET isotopes emit just one photon at a time. In each case, the photons are recorded by detectors arrayed around the head. PET is superior to SPET because smaller changes can be detected and more accurately pinpointed. The safest technique is functional magnetic resonance (fMR) blood-oxygen-level dependent (BOLD) imaging. This produces a map of rCBF and brain activity, from the natural change in paramagnetic properties of hemoglobin as it deoxygenates. Initial problems of low resolution and movement artefacts with fMR have been overcome, and this is now the most widely used functional imaging approach.

53

TABLE 7.3

Comparing functional brain imaging techniques

	Single-photon emission tomography	Positron emission tomography	Functional magnetic resonance	Magnetic resonance spectroscopy imaging
Availability	+++	+	+++	++
Safety	+	++	+++	+++
Spatial resolution	6 mm	3 mm	3 mm	5 mm
Time resolution	Hours	Minutes	Seconds	Minutes
Sensitivity	+	+++	++	++
Parameters measured	Regional cerebral blood flow Receptor density and binding	Regional cerebral blood flow Receptor density Glucose metabolism	Regional cerebral blood flow	Selected biochemistry (e.g. phosphate)
Drawbacks	High radiation levels	Expensive	Sensitive to movement artefact	Strong magnetic fields are best

+, little advantage for this technique
+++, strong advantage for this technique

Magnetic resonance spectroscopy (MRS) allows the assessment of brain biochemistry. 31-phosphorus MRS shows a series of peaks, which correspond to energy reactions in the cell, involving ATP, as well as turnover of membranes in synapses and vesicles (Figure 7.1). In untreated schizophrenia, MRS of the prefrontal cortex has repeatedly shown a decrease in phosphomonoesters and an increase in phosphodiesters. This suggests a decreased synthesis and/or increased breakdown of cell membrane phospholipids, which might reflect

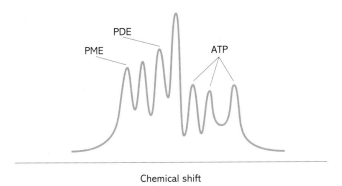

Chemical shift

Figure 7.1 31-phosphorus MR spectroscopy for assessment of brain biochemistry. ATP, adenosine triphosphate; PDE, phosphodiesters; PME, phosphomonoesters.

disturbed pruning of synapses. Proton MRS visualizes a separate set of biochemical processes and suggests reduced frontal glutamate activity in early schizophrenia. One current hypothesis suggests that this reduced glutamate activity turns into increased activity at the onset of the illness, with excitatory damage leading to synaptic loss and longer-term progression of the illness.

Experimental design

Imaging brain function is more difficult than imaging brain structure. Ensuring that patients and controls are engaged in similar standardized cognitive activity is usually important, to reduce chance variations and allow real differences to be seen. Unless they are properly controlled for, drug effects can mask all other effects.

A common method of investigating the abnormal brain function underpinning a cognitive deficit is to first scan a normal subject before and during the execution of a relevant task. By subtracting the brain activity map as it was before the task from the map during the task, the specific areas of the brain involved in the task will be highlighted. The same brain activity maps are then produced for patients before and during the same task, which can then be compared with the pattern in normal subjects. A general finding is that patients with schizophrenia tend to use aberrant networks of cortical activity even during simple cognitive, perceptual, or motor tasks and even when performance is apparently normal.

Image analysis is challenging. Either functional images have to be mapped precisely onto structural scans ('co-registration') or images from groups of subjects are transformed into identical brain shapes with differences between groups then expressed as maps of significant p scores (e.g. those of $p < 0.01$). This is called statistical parametric mapping.

Mapping symptoms

Functional imaging has been informative at the level of understanding individual symptoms, symptom clusters and specific cognitive deficits in schizophrenia (Figure 7.2). The three overlapping syndromes outlined in Chapter 2 correlate with particular cognitive deficits and with distinct patterns of brain function (Tables 7.4 and 7.5). Negative symptoms, or the psychomotor poverty syndrome, correlate with decreased activity in the dorsolateral prefrontal cortex, particularly on the left. Interestingly, this pattern also appears in severe depressive illness with psychomotor retardation, thus indicating a final common cortical deficit underlying psychomotor poverty in schizophrenia and psychomotor retardation in depression.

Among positive symptoms, auditory hallucinations, rather than delusions, have been most extensively studied. This is partly because the normal cerebral mechanisms of auditory perception are well understood, but the normal mechanisms underlying the formation of beliefs are not. During auditory hallucinations, increased blood flow is seen in Broca's area in the left hemisphere. This is similar to the activity produced during normal speech and during normal 'inner' speech, when one is rehearsing something silently to oneself. In a healthy brain, a connected area of cortex in the superior temporal gyrus is deactivated during inner speech. Functional imaging shows this not to occur in hallucinating patients, suggesting that hallucinations may actually be misinterpreted inner speech.

In some cases, the link between a specific symptom and a functional abnormality emerges only under particular conditions. Compared with controls, patients with persecutory delusions show increased activation

TABLE 7.4

Functional imaging: how symptoms and brain activity correlate

Symptom	Brain regions involved	Activity change compared with normal
Negative symptoms / psychomotor poverty	Left dorsolateral prefrontal cortex	Decrease
	Inferior parietal cortex	Decrease
Auditory hallucinations	Broca's area	Increase
	Superior temporal gyrus	Fails to decrease
	Parahippocampal region	Decrease
Total positive symptoms	Hippocampal region	Increase
Formal thought disorder	Wernicke's area	Decrease
Persecutory delusions	Amygdala	Increase
Passivity experiences	Cingulate gyrus	Increase
	Right parietal	Increase

TABLE 7.5

Functional imaging of cognitive deficits in schizophrenia

Cognitive deficit in	Failure of normal activation in
Working memory	Dorsolateral prefrontal cortex
Verbal fluency	Left dorsolateral prefrontal cortex
	Failure to deactivate superior temporal cortex
Error monitoring	Anterior cingulate gyrus
Olfaction	Insula
	Parahippocampal gyrus
Inhibition of reflex eye saccades	Striatum

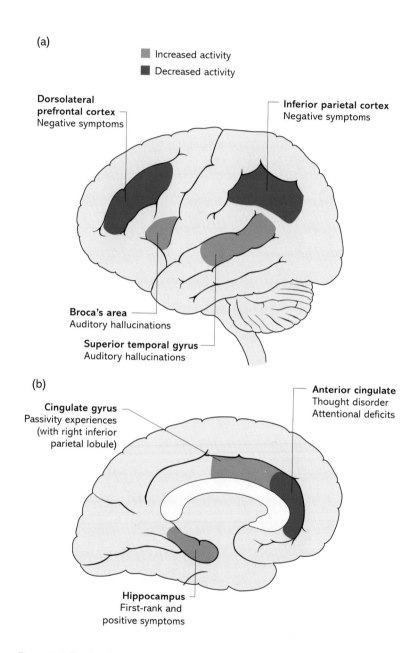

Figure 7.2 The localization of psychotic symptoms and deficits in the brain, as shown by functional imaging studies: (a) lateral view of left hemisphere; (b) medial view of left hemisphere.

in the amygdala in situations of possible threat. Patients with auditory hallucinations show right-sided temporoparietal and parahippocampal deficits during inner speech tasks, again suggesting an internal monitoring problem.

Neuropsychology and functional imaging – Key points

- Patients with schizophrenia exhibit subtle neurocognitive impairments prior to the onset of florid psychotic symptoms.
- Family and twin studies suggest that several neurocognitive impairments may be present in non-affected family members.
- Neurocognitive impairments are a major determinant of poor social and occupational functioning.
- Negative symptoms correlate with decreased metabolic activity in the dorsolateral prefrontal cortex.
- Auditory hallucinations are associated with increased blood flow in Broca's area in the left hemisphere.
- Formal thought disorder is associated with decreased activity in Wernicke's area.

Key references

Buchanan RW, Strauss ME, Kirkpatrick B et al. Neuro-psychological impairments in deficit vs. nondeficit forms of schizophrenia. *Arch Gen Psychiatry* 1994;51: 804–11.

Crespo-Facorro B, Paradiso S, Andreasen N et al. Neural mechanisms of anhedonia in schizophrenia: a PET study of response to unpleasant and pleasant odors. *JAMA* 2001;286:427–35.

Freedman R, Adler LE, Myles-Worsley M et al. Inhibitory gating of an evoked response to repeated auditory stimuli in schizophrenic and normal subjects. *Arch Gen Psychiatry* 1996;53:114–21.

Frith CD, Friston KJ, Silbersweig D et al. Regional brain activity in chronic schizophrenic patients during a verbal fluency task. *Br J Psychiatry* 1995;167: 343–9.

Goldberg TE, Gold JM. Neurocognitive functioning in patients with schizophrenia: an overview. In Bloom FE, Kupfer DJ, eds. *Psychopharmacology: The Fourth Generation of Progress.* New York: Raven Press, 1995:1245–7.

Green MF. What are the functional consequences of neurocognitive deficits in schizophrenia? *Am J Psychiatry* 1996;153:321–30.

Kircher TT, Liddle PF, Brammer M et al. Neural correlates of formal thought disorder in schizophrenia: preliminary findings from a functional magnetic resonance imaging study. *Arch Gen Psychiatry* 2001;58:769–74

Levy DL, Holzman PS, Matthysse S, Mendell NR. Eye tracking and schizophrenia: a selective review. *Schizophr Bull* 1994;20:47–62.

Liddle PF, Friston KJ, Frith CD et al. Patterns of cerebral blood flow in schizophrenia. *Br J Psychiatry* 1992;160:179–86.

McGuire PK, Silbersweig DA, Wright I et al. Abnormal monitoring of inner speech: a physiological basis for auditory hallucinations. *Lancet* 1995;346:596–600.

Norman RMG, Malla AK, Morrison-Stewart SL et al. Neuropsychological correlates of syndromes in schizophrenia. *Br J Psychiatry* 1997;170:134–9.

Perlstein WM, Carter CS, Cohen JD. Relation of prefrontal cortex dysfunction to working memory and symptoms in schizophrenia. *Am J Psychiatry* 2001;158:1105–13.

Raemaekers M, Jansma JM, Cahn W et al. Neuronal substrate of the saccadic inhibition deficit in schizophrenia investigated with 3D event-related fMRI. *Arch Gen Psychiatry* 2002;59:313–20.

Silbersweig DA, Stern E, Frith CD et al. A functional neuroanatomy of auditory hallucinations in schizophrenia. *Nature* 1995;378:176.

Spence SA, Brooks DJ, Hirsch SR et al. A PET study of voluntary movements in schizophrenic patients experiencing passivity phenomena. *Brain* 1997;120:1997–2011.

Spence SA, Liddle PF, Stefan MD et al. Functional anatomy of verbal fluency in people with schizophrenia and those at genetic risk. Focal dysfunction and distributed disconnectivity revisited. *Br J Psychiatry* 2000;176:47–51.

Tek C, Gold J, Blaxton T et al. Visual perceptual and working memory impairments in schizophrenia. *Arch Gen Psychiatry* 2002;59:146–51.

Thaker GK, Ross DE, Cassady SL et al. Saccadic eye movement abnormalities in relatives of patients with schizophrenia. *Schizophr Res* 2000;45:235–44.

Neurochemical abnormalities are the link between underlying causal factors, either genetic or environmental, and the overt expression of signs and symptoms of the illness. Over the last four decades, multiple neurotransmitter systems have been hypothesized to be involved in the neurochemistry of schizophrenia. These hypotheses have fallen in and out of vogue as our knowledge of the brain and our methods for investigating brain neurobiology have become more sophisticated. The major neurochemical pathophysiological hypotheses continue to involve the traditional neurotransmitters, though this situation will likely change over the next decade as findings emerge from the application of novel molecular biological techniques to the study of schizophrenia.

The dopamine hypothesis

Dopamine cell bodies exist in two areas: the hypothalamus and the midbrain. In the hypothalamus, dopamine controls pituitary prolactin release (tuberohypophyseal pathway). The midbrain is the source of three pathways: one from the substantia nigra to the dorsal striatum in the basal ganglia (nigrostriatal pathway), and two others projecting from the ventral tegmental area to the ventral striatum (mesolimbic pathway) and to the frontal cortex (mesocortical pathway) (Figure 8.1).

In the early 1960s, Arvid Carlsson posited the dopamine hypothesis of schizophrenia, in which he stated that schizophrenia was due to an excess of dopaminergic activity: an excess of dopamine release and/or hypersensitivity of dopamine receptors. The hypothesis was supported by several observations. First was the recognition of a schizophrenia-like psychosis in people who misused amphetamine, a drug known to increase the release of dopamine. Second was the emergence of side-effects of the recently discovered antipsychotic chlorpromazine, which mimicked Parkinson's disease, itself thought to be due to faulty dopamine transmission. Third was the observation that all drugs that were effective antipsychotic agents were dopamine receptor antagonists. In the following 15 years, several experiments provided compelling but

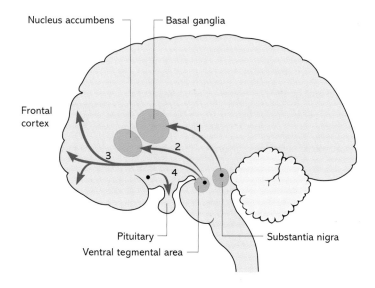

Figure 8.1 Dopamine pathways in the brain: (1) nigrostriatal; (2) mesolimbic; (3) mesocortical; (4) tuberohypophyseal.

circumstantial evidence in further support of the importance of dopamine D_2 activity in schizophrenia. However, there were known shortcomings in the dopamine hypothesis and direct evidence was lacking. In addition, the prediction that untreated patients should have increased numbers of dopamine receptors received no firm support from postmortem assays nor, more critically, from PET studies which imaged the binding of radiolabeled antipsychotic drugs to receptors.

Three developments helped to revive the dopamine hypothesis. First, the hypothesis was reformulated to predict the existence of both hyperdopaminergic and hypodopaminergic activity in schizophrenic patients. Positive symptoms are due to increased activity of the mesolimbic dopamine pathway (see Figure 8.1), whereas negative symptoms are due to decreased activity of the mesocortical dopamine pathway. Second, in the late 1980s, new molecular-biological techniques found five dopamine receptor subtypes. They differ functionally and in their pattern of target neuron / brain region

TABLE 8.1

Target neuron location of dopamine receptor subtypes

Location	Receptor subtype
Basal ganglia	D_1, D_2
Nucleus accumbens	D_2, D_3
Frontal cortex, hippocampus	D_1, D_4, D_5

distribution (Table 8.1). D_1 receptors are the most common and are always postsynaptic. D_5 is related. The D_2 family includes D_2, D_3 and D_4. D_2 receptors are located both presynaptically on dopamine terminals, where they act as autoreceptors regulating dopamine release, and postsynaptically. The future elucidation of the role of the other new dopamine receptors may lead to further modifications of the hypothesis. Third, more informative functional imaging approaches have been developed for assessing in-vivo dopamine activity. One approach is based on the infusion of a subject with an indirect dopamine agonist. The extent to which radioligand occupancy of postsynaptic dopamine receptors is reduced by competition with the increased endogenous dopamine is then determined. The comparison of pre- and postinfusion radioligand occupancy provides an index of dopamine release and reuptake rates. Studies using this approach have documented increased dopamine release in patients with schizophrenia compared with normal controls, and suggest that the extent of dopamine release is associated with the severity of positive psychotic symptoms. The other approach has examined the relationship of dopamine D_2 receptor occupancy of antipsychotic medications and the occurrence of symptom remission and side-effects. These studies have shown a strong association among dopamine D_2 receptor occupancy, antipsychotic dose, symptom remission and side-effects.

Although the dopamine hypothesis remains the most salient hypothesis, there is still the issue that a significant proportion of patients with schizophrenia do not adequately respond to dopamine antagonists, which suggests that other neurotransmitters are involved in the pathophysiology of schizophrenia.

Does serotonin play a role?

Serotonergic neurons project from the raphé nucleus in the brainstem to basal ganglia, limbic, thalamic and cortical regions throughout the brain (Figure 8.2). As with dopamine, several families of serotonin (5-HT) receptors have now been identified (Table 8.2). 5-HT was proposed as an important transmitter in schizophrenia before the dopamine hypothesis, mainly because of the psychotomimetic properties of lysergic acid diethylamide (LSD), which releases 5-HT. However, no direct supporting evidence has been found; only recently, in the light of the potent 5-HT$_{2a}$ receptor antagonism of clozapine and the other new-generation antipsychotics, have 5-HT mechanisms been seriously considered.

The ratio of 5-HT$_{2a}$ to D$_2$ blockade has been proposed as the critical distinction between conventional and new-generation antipsychotic drugs (see Chapter 9 for a review of these drugs). The affinity of clozapine for the 5-HT$_{2a}$ receptor exceeds its affinity for D$_2$ receptors 20-fold, although some conventional antipsychotics, such as chlorpromazine, also have greater affinity for the 5-HT$_{2a}$ receptor than for the D$_2$ receptor. One possible explanation of the therapeutic role of

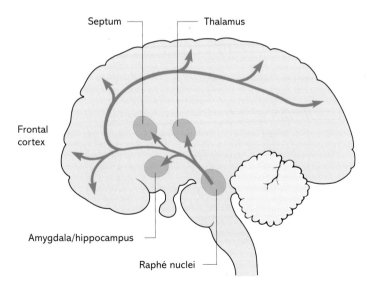

Septum —   — Thalamus

Frontal cortex

Amygdala/hippocampus —

Raphé nuclei —

Figure 8.2 Serotonin pathways in the brain.

TABLE 8.2

Human brain 5-HT receptors and their actions

Receptor	Action
5-HT$_1$	5-HT$_{1a}$ receptors are involved in anxiolytic/antidepressant actions
	5-HT$_{1b}$ receptors are involved in aggression
	5-HT$_{1d}$ and 5-HT$_{1e}$ receptors: functional role unclear
	5-HT$_{1f}$ receptors are involved in migraine
5-HT$_2$	5-HT$_{2a}$ receptors modulate ascending dopamine pathways
	5-HT$_{2c}$ receptors are involved in hunger
	Mescaline and LSD are 5-HT$_2$ agonists
5-HT$_3$	Found in limbic and frontal cortex
	May be involved in aggression
5-HT$_4$	May be involved in cognition and anxiety
5-HT$_5$	Functional role unclear
5-HT$_6$	May be involved in depression
5HT$_7$	May be involved in circadian rhythm and epilepsy

5-HT$_{2a}$ blockade is that it stimulates dopamine activity in the mesocortical pathways without causing the mesolimbic stimulation that underlies positive symptoms.

Postmortem studies have suggested fewer 5-HT$_{2a}$ receptors in the frontal and temporal cortex, and reduced 5-HT$_{2a}$ gene expression in the frontal cortex, in patients with schizophrenia compared with normal controls. However, treatment studies with selective 5-HT$_{2a}$ antagonists have not been encouraging, and functional imaging studies with 5-HT ligands have not been able to consistently replicate the observation of decreased 5-HT$_{2a}$ receptors in the prefrontal cortex.

Possible role of glutamate?
Glutamate is the major excitatory neurotransmitter in the central nervous system and plays a central role in cortical–subcortical and

thalamic–cortical excitatory projections. Glutamate acts at both metabotropic and ionotropic receptors. Developmental abnormalities in glutamate release have been hypothesized to cause underactivity of the N-methyl-D-aspartate (NMDA) ionotropic receptor in patients with schizophrenia. There is indirect evidence to support this hypothesis. Phencyclidine (PCP) causes a psychosis that has been described as including both positive and negative symptoms. PCP exerts its effect through blocking the ion channel gated by the NMDA-type glutamate receptor, which would produce a hypoglutamatergic state. Long-term PCP administration results in depletion of prefrontal dopamine. The decreased glutamatergic activity could produce negative symptoms either directly through decreased prefrontal cortical input and output or indirectly through the secondary decrease in prefrontal dopaminergic activity. A different mechanism would underlie its psychotomimetic effects.

There is accumulating evidence to support a glutamate hypothesis. Postmortem studies have documented abnormal NMDA and kainate and AMPA (the other two ionotropic receptors) receptor binding in the prefrontal and temporal cortex, and abnormal NMDA and AMPA mRNA receptor expression in the hippocampus. Perhaps the most compelling evidence comes from clinical trials that have examined the efficacy of agents that modify the activity of the NMDA receptor. These studies have shown that glycine, D-serine and D-cycloserine, which bind to the glycine site of the NMDA receptor, may be effective treatments for negative symptoms.

What about acetylcholine?

Acetylcholine acts at muscarinic and nicotinic cholinergic receptors. These receptors are broadly distributed throughout the brain, including the neocortex, hippocampus and basal ganglia. Acetylcholine modulates the release of a number of different neurotransmitters, including glutamate and dopamine. Cholinergic mechanisms have been implicated in the regulation of attention, memory, processing speed and sensory gating processes – processes which are impaired in patients with schizophrenia. Further, nicotine has previously been shown to improve eye-tracking and sensory gating, as measured by P50, in patients with schizophrenia. Future studies are required to delineate the role of acetylcholine in schizophrenia.

Other neurotransmitters

Gamma-aminobutyric acid (GABA), norepinephrine and neuropeptides are additional neurotransmitters that have been hypothesized to be involved in the pathophysiology of schizophrenia. The multitude of neurochemical hypotheses points to both the possibility of multiple neurotransmitter systems being affected and the lack of definitive evidence for any one system.

Neurochemistry – Key points

- The dopamine hypothesis remains the major neurochemical hypothesis of schizophrenia.
- Positive symptoms are hypothesized to be due to increased activity of the mesolimbic dopamine pathway.
- Negative symptoms are hypothesized to be due to decreased activity of the mesocortical dopamine pathway.
- Decreased glutamate activity may be involved in the pathophysiology of negative symptoms.
- Disturbances in the cholinergic system have been hypothesized to underlie cognitive impairments in schizophrenia.

Key references

Carlsson A, Waters N, Carlsson ML. Neurotransmitter interactions in schizophrenia—therapeutic implications. *Biol Psychiatry* 1999;46:1388–95.

Creese I, Burt DR, Snyder SH. Dopamine receptor binding predicts clinical and pharmacological potencies of antischizophrenic drugs. *Science* 1976;192:481–3.

Dolan RJ, Fletcher P, Frith CD et al. Dopaminergic modulation of impaired cognitive activation in the anterior cingulate cortex in schizophrenia. *Nature* 1995;378:180–2.

Farber NB, Newcomer JW, Olney JW. Glycine agonists: what can they teach us about schizophrenia? *Arch Gen Psychiatry* 1999;56:13–17.

Farde L, Wiesel F-A, Stone-Elander S et al. D_2 dopamine receptors in neuroleptic-naive schizophrenic patients. *Arch Gen Psychiatry* 1990;47:213–19.

Javitt DC, Zukin SR. Recent advances in the phencyclidine model of schizophrenia. *Am J Psychiatry* 1991;148:1301–8.

The modern era of the pharmacological treatment of schizophrenia began in the early 1950s with the discovery that chlorpromazine (thorazine) had antipsychotic properties. The introduction and eventual widespread use of chlorpromazine and other antipsychotics has facilitated a major paradigm shift in the treatment of the patient with schizophrenia, from a hospital-based to a community-based system of care.

There are two major classes of antipsychotic medications: conventional, traditional or typical antipsychotics or neuroleptics; and new-generation, novel or atypical antipsychotics. Antipsychotic medications constitute the primary class of drugs used to treat schizophrenia.

Conventional antipsychotics

The majority of conventional antipsychotics have a similar mechanism of action, and they are all potent dopamine D_2 receptor antagonists. This property is hypothesized to be the basis of their antipsychotic action. There are five major classes of these drugs (see Table 9.1). There are both oral and injectable, long-acting depot forms of antipsychotics. Their primary indication is for positive symptoms, i.e. hallucinations, delusions and positive formal thought disorder. They have limited use for either negative symptoms or the cognitive impairments in patients with schizophrenia. In the treatment of acute psychotic episodes, these drugs will usually begin to improve symptoms within the first week. Improvement will continue to accrue over the following few months of treatment, with most improvement occurring during the first 6 weeks of treatment. The usual dosage of a conventional antipsychotic for the treatment of an acute episode should be in the range 300–1000 chlorpromazine equivalents (CPZE)/day, where 100 CPZE is the dose equivalent in effect to 100 mg of chlorpromazine (see Table 9.1).

TABLE 9.1

Conventional antipsychotics

Class	Generic name	Chlorpromazine equivalents of commonly used drugs
Phenothiazines	Chlorpromazine	100 mg
	Mesoridazine*	50 mg
	Thioridazine*	100 mg
	Fluphenazine	2 mg
	Perphenazine	10 mg
	Trifluoperazine	5 mg
Thioxanthenes	Thiothixene*	5 mg
Butyrophenones	Haloperidol	2 mg
Dibenzoxazepines	Loxapine	10 mg
Dihydroindolones	Molindone*	10 mg

*Not licensed in UK at time of press

Conventional antipsychotics are also indicated for the maintenance phase of treatment. Maintenance treatment is designed to suppress psychotic symptomatology and/or prevent the reoccurrence of a psychotic episode. The maintenance dosage of a conventional antipsychotic should be in the range 300–600 CPZE/day.

A major problem in the maintenance treatment of a patient with schizophrenia is lack of adherence to the recommended pharmacological treatment regimen. The depot forms of conventional antipsychotics are particularly useful in this regard, because they can be administered once every 2–6 weeks, and relieve the patient and carer of the burden of remembering to take medications daily. Depot preparations are used relatively frequently in the UK, but tend to be underused in the USA.

Side-effects. Conventional antipsychotics have a broad range of side-effects. The most important of these are extrapyramidal side-effects (EPS), e.g. akinesia, dystonia and tremor. The side-effect profile of an antipsychotic is largely related to its potency or strength. High-potency antipsychotics (e.g. haloperidol, fluphenazine) are more likely to cause EPS, whereas low-potency antipsychotics (e.g. chlorpromazine, thioridazine) are more likely to cause sedation and orthostatic hypotension. EPS constitute a major cause of non-adherence to treatment. High-potency antipsychotics are also more likely to cause neuroleptic malignant syndrome (NMS), a syndrome characterized by muscle rigidity, autonomic instability (e.g. elevated pulse rate and blood pressure), fever and mental status changes. NMS is relatively rare (incidence less than 1%) but, if left untreated, is associated with a relatively high mortality rate.

The other major side-effect associated with all conventional antipsychotics is tardive dyskinesia (TD). TD is characterized by abnormal, involuntary movements and primarily affects the muscles of the tongue and face. It may also involve the muscles of the extremities, pelvic girdle and/or the diaphragm. TD varies in severity, with the majority of cases being relatively mild, but severe cases can be quite disabling and lead to marked functional impairments. The cumulative incidence of conventional antipsychotic-induced TD is about 5% of patients per year of treatment.

New-generation antipsychotics

The new-generation, or atypical, antipsychotics (see Tables 9.2 and 9.3) were developed in an attempt to find effective antipsychotics with minimal potential for causing either EPS or TD. Unlike conventional antipsychotics, these agents are usually also potent $5HT_{2a}$ receptor antagonists. They may also have noradrenergic, histaminergic and cholinergic antagonistic effects.

Clozapine. The first new-generation antipsychotic was clozapine. Although originally developed in the early 1960s, clozapine was not marketed in the UK and USA until 1990, because of concerns about the increased occurrence of agranulocytosis. In addition to its potent serotonergic $5HT_{2a}$ receptor antagonist activity, clozapine differs from conventional antipsychotics in its relative potency at the dopamine D_1 and D_4 receptors. Any one of these properties may be related to its superior efficacy for positive symptoms. Clozapine is the only new-

TABLE 9.2

Relative indications for the new and older antipsychotic drugs

New-generation / atypical antipsychotics

- First- and second-line treatments
- Patients intolerant of conventional antipsychotic side-effects, e.g. neurological or endocrine side-effects
- Patients with refractory positive symptoms (clozapine)

Conventional antipsychotics

- Patients who are non-adherent: long-acting depot preparations
- During pregnancy
- Third- or fourth-line treatments
- If cost is a priority

generation antipsychotic that has been approved for the treatment of positive symptoms resistant to conventional antipsychotics. It is also effective for alleviating negative symptoms secondary to positive symptoms, EPS or dysphoric affect. Clozapine has not been shown to be effective for primary negative symptoms. It has been found to reduce suicidal ideation in schizophrenia.

Although clozapine causes few EPS and little TD, it does have a number of side-effects that limit its utilization. The most serious of these is agranulocytosis, which occurs in up to 1% of treated patients, may be life-threatening and necessitates regular blood monitoring. However, the most clinically important side-effects may be the significant weight gain and disruptions of glucose and lipid metabolism that are associated with clozapine treatment. Clozapine has been shown to be responsible for the induction of new cases of Type 2 diabetes mellitus. These drawbacks underscore the principle that all medications are associated with side-effects and that the decreased occurrence of one serious set of side-effects may be offset by the increased occurrence of an equally serious set of others. Other common clozapine side-effects include sedation, sialorrhea and seizures.

TABLE 9.3

New-generation antipsychotic drugs and their side-effects

Drug	Main adverse effects	Comment
Clozapine	Agranulocytosis (reduced risk with regular monitoring) Sedation Seizures Salivation Weight gain Hyperlipidemias Diabetes mellitus	The only new-generation antipsychotic effective for refractory positive symptoms: clinical improvement in 30–60%
Risperidone	Insomnia, agitation EPS at higher doses Prolactin elevation	Evidence for enhanced relapse prevention
Olanzapine	Headache Sedation Weight gain Hyperlipidemias Diabetes mellitus	Few EPS
Quetiapine	Sedation Postural hypotension Dizziness Constipation	Few or no EPS
Amisulpride	Prolactin elevation EPS at higher doses	D_2 and D_3 specific
Ziprasadone	Insomnia EPS at higher doses Possible cardiac Q–Tc interval effects	Weight neutral
Aripiprazole	Mild dose-related EPS	Partial D_2 agonist Long half-life

Other new-generation antipsychotics. The other new-generation antipsychotics share with clozapine potent 5-HT_{2a} antagonist properties, but differ in the degree to which they share the other pharmacological properties of clozapine. Several of the new-generation antipsychotics are known to cause significant weight gain, disruption of glucose and lipid metabolism, and cardiac conduction abnormalities. They share with clozapine the reduced proclivity for causing EPS and TD. This latter property has led to their supplanting the conventional antipsychotics as first-line treatments for acute psychotic episodes and maintenance therapy. However, none of the other new-generation antipsychotics has yet been shown to be as effective as clozapine for treatment-resistant positive symptoms. Their putative efficacy for negative symptoms has not been sufficiently investigated to determine whether any of these new drugs are effective for both primary and secondary negative symptoms.

Treatment of negative symptoms

The treatment of negative symptoms is a major challenge facing clinicians. Conventional and new-generation antipsychotics are relatively effective for treating secondary negative symptoms, but leave untouched the primary avolitional syndrome described so eloquently by Kraepelin (see Chapter 1). The limited efficacy of antipsychotics has led to the investigation of alternative treatments for negative symptoms. Various approaches have been attempted based on specific neurochemical hypotheses of the pathophysiology of negative symptoms (see Table 9.4). One of the more recent strategies that has

TABLE 9.4

Pharmacological strategies for the treatment of negative symptoms

Dopaminergic agents	Serotonergic agents
• L-dopa	• Fluoxetine
• D-amphetamine	• Fluvoxamine
• Bromocriptine	• Ritanserin
• Mazindol	
Noradrenergic agents	**Glutamatergic agents**
• Propranolol	• D-cycloserine
• Clonidine	• Glycine
	• D-serine

received some empirical support is the use of agents that act at the glycine site of the N-methyl-D-aspartate (NMDA) glutamate receptor. This approach is based on the proposition that negative symptoms are secondary to decreased glutamatergic activity. In preliminary studies, glycine, D-serine and D-cycloserine have been shown to be effective in ameliorating persistent negative symptoms. Whether this therapeutic effect includes primary negative symptoms needs to be determined.

Treatment of cognitive impairments

Conventional antipsychotics have limited effects on the cognitive impairments of schizophrenia. Acute treatment may worsen reaction time, whereas chronic treatment has been shown to improve attention. New-generation antipsychotics may have modest benefits for multiple cognitive processes, but whether this represents a direct cognitive enhancing effect or an indirect effect mediated through decreased adverse effects has not been established. Regardless, patients continue to exhibit pronounced cognitive impairments despite adequate new-generation antipsychotic treatment.

Adjunctive treatments

Despite the advent of clozapine, a large percentage of patients continue to experience significant residual positive symptoms. A number of agents have been used in combination with onging antipsychotic treatment in an attempt to alleviate these symptoms. The agents most commonly used in this regard are antiseizure medications (e.g. carbamazepine), antidepressants, benzodiazepines and lithium. However, although there are reports of small subgroups of patients who may benefit from combination therapy with one of these agents, there has not been a consistent demonstration of enhanced positive symptom efficacy when these drugs have been used in combination with antipsychotics. Rather, these drugs may be more effective when used to treat patients with persistent symptoms of anxiety, depression, hostility or mania. Reports of enhanced response to clozapine when the glutamate-active anticonvulsant lamotrigine is administered appear promising.

Pharmacological treatment – Key points

- The depot forms of conventional antipsychotics are useful for patients who are non-adherent to their medications.
- Clozapine is the only new-generation antipsychotic that is effective for positive symptoms resistant to conventional antipsychotics.
- New-generation antipsychotics other than clozapine have become the first-line treatments for acute psychotic episodes and maintenance therapy.
- Conventional and new-generation antipsychotics are relatively effective for treating secondary, but not primary, negative symptoms.
- Conventional antipsychotics have limited effects on the cognitive impairments of schizophrenia.
- New-generation antipsychotics may have modest benefits for multiple cognitive processes.

Key references

Bilder RM, Goldman RS, Volavka J et al. Neurocognitive effects of clozapine, olanzapine, risperidone, and haloperidol in patients with chronic schizophrenia or schizoaffective disorder. *Am J Psychiatry* 2002;159:1018–28.

Carpenter Jr WT, Breier A, Buchanan RW et al. Mazindol treatment of negative symptoms. *Neuropsychopharmacology* 2000;23:365–74.

Copolov DL, Link CG, Kowalcyk B. A multicentre, double-blind, randomized comparison of quetiapine (ICI 204,636, 'Seroquel') and haloperidol in schizophrenia. *Psychol Med* 2000;30:95–105.

Daniel DG, Zimbroff DL, Potkin SG et al. Ziprasidone 80 mg/day and 160 mg/day in the acute exacerbation of schizophrenia and schizoaffective disorder: a 6-week placebo-controlled trial. Ziprasidone Study Group. *Neuropsychopharmacology* 1999;20(5):491–505.

Dixon LB, Lehman AF, Levine J. Conventional antipsychotic medications for schizophrenia. *Schizophr Bull* 1995;21:567–77.

Goff DC, Tsai G, Levitt J et al. A placebo-controlled trial of D-cycloserine added to conventional neuroleptics in patients with schizophrenia. *Arch Gen Psychiatry* 1999;56(1):21–7.

Heresco-Levy U, Javitt DC, Ermilov M et al. Efficacy of high-dose glycine in the treatment of enduring negative symptoms of schizophrenia. *Arch Gen Psychiatry* 1999;56(1):29–36.

Johns CA, Thompson JW. Adjunctive treatments in schizophrenia. *Schizophr Bull* 1995;21:607–19.

Kane JM. Schizophrenia. *N Engl J Med* 1996;334:34.

Kane JM, Honigfeld G, Singer J, Meltzer H. Clozapine for the treatment-resistant schizophrenia: a double-blind comparison with chlorpromazine. *Arch Gen Psychiatry* 1988;45:789–96.

Kane JM, Marder SR, Schooler NR et al. Clozapine and haloperidol in moderately refractory schizophrenia. *Arch Gen Psychiatry* 2001;58: 965–72.

Kane JR, Schooler NR, Marder S et al. Efficacy of clozapine versus haloperidol in a long-term clinical trial. *Schizophr Res* 1996;18:127.

Lawler CP, Prioleau C, Lewis MM et al. Interactions of the novel antipsychotic aripiprazole with dopamine and serotonin receptor subtypes. *Neuropsychopharmacology* 1999;20:612–27.

Marder SR, Meibach RC. Risperidone in the treatment of schizophrenia. *Am J Psychiatry* 1994;151:1825–35.

Meltzer HY, Okali G. The reduction of suicidality during clozapine treatment in neuroleptic resistant schizophrenia: impact on risk–benefit assessment. *Am J Psychiatry* 1995;152:183–90.

Purdon SE, Jones BD, Stip E et al. Neuropsychological change in early phase schizophrenia during 12 months of treatment with olanzapine, risperidone, or haloperidol. *Arch Gen Psychiatry* 2000;57(3):249–58.

Peuskens J. Risperidone in the treatment of patients with chronic schizophrenia: a multi-national, multi-centre, double-blind, parallel-group study versus haloperidol. *Br J Psychiatry* 1995;166:712–26.

Rosenheck R, Tekell J, Peters J et al. Does participation in social treatment augment the benefit of clozapine? *Arch Gen Psychiatry* 1998;55: 618–25.

Tollefson GD, Beasley CM, Tran PV et al. Olanzapine versus haloperidol in the treatment of schizophrenia and schizoaffective and schizophreniform disorders: results of an international collaborative trial. *Am J Psychiatry* 1997;154:457–65.

Small JG, Hirsch SR, Arvanitis LA et al. and the Seroquel Study Group. Quetiapine in patients with schizophrenia. *Arch Gen Psychiatry* 1997;54:549–57.

10 Psychosocial interventions and non-drug treatments

Psychosocial interventions have been a key part of the management of schizophrenia since the 1970s. At that time, the adverse impact of institutionalization on people with schizophrenia came to be realized, and this led to the increased development of community-based services. More recently, specific psychological techniques aimed at improving aspects of schizophrenia have also been evaluated (Table 10.1).

Modern service settings

Multidisciplinary teams are the core of community-based services for people with schizophrenia. These are effective when a case management model is used, so that one care coordinator develops and oversees the patient's full care package. Different models of care management exist, but systematic reviews have shown that it is most effective when combined with assertive community treatment. This involves proactive community follow-up and delivery of as much care as possible in the home setting of the patient. Getting patients back to work is important. Systematic review has shown that supported employment programs,

TABLE 10.1

Effective psychological treatments in schizophrenia

Treatment	Evidence base: number of good randomized trials
Family intervention	7
Cognitive therapy for persistent symptoms	4
Cognitive therapy for acute symptoms	2
Motivational interventions in dual diagnosis	1
Compliance therapy	1
Cognitive remediation for chronic disabilities	1

in which a patient is put into a real job and supported actively, outperform traditional sheltered employment approaches. Specialist rehabilitation services aim to reduce the enduring deficits in chronic schizophrenia and improve day-to-day social functioning.

Family interventions

The concept of high family 'expressed emotion' as an environmental predictor of relapse in schizophrenia was suggested in the 1960s by Brown and Rutter. Families who showed over-involvement or excessive criticism were associated with high relapse rates in schizophrenic individuals. Whether the high expressed emotion was the cause of the poor prognosis, or partly the effect of illness severity, has not been resolved. Nevertheless, family-based interventions aimed at enhancing coping strategies by education about the illness (Table 10.2) have been shown to improve prognosis. A meta-analysis of the best randomized controlled trials, with a collective total of 350 patients and their families, found that such interventions, usually delivered over 9 months, were both effective and cost-effective. Patients who had family interventions showed lower relapse rates and improved drug compliance. Families valued the treatment and experienced less burden of care. This effect appears to be enduring and can be delivered to groups of families, with some evidence that this is the most cost-effective method. Family support combined with individual psychological techniques has been shown to reduce relapse rates in schizophrenia complicated by substance misuse.

TABLE 10.2

Components of an effective family intervention

- Engage families soon after acute admission
- Videos and seminars to educate the family about schizophrenia
- Early intervention in threatened relapse
- Teach problem-solving techniques

Psychological treatment of positive symptoms

The idea that cognitive–behavioral treatments that are effective in major depression might be effective in treating positive psychotic symptoms is relatively new. Traditionally, these symptoms have been viewed, in the words of the phenomenologist Jaspers, as 'un-understandable'. This, coupled with the failure of psychoanalytical treatments for schizophrenia in the 1950s and 1960s, left a legacy of skepticism about psychological approaches.

Recent trials have shown that cognitive–behavior therapy (CBT) can be effective for persistent psychotic symptoms in chronic schizophrenia when given in addition to routine care. The effect size in four large, independent randomized controlled trials is about the same as that for clozapine. Components of this technique are shown in Table 10.3. Which of these components are the most important remains to be clarified. Recent trials have also shown that these techniques, added to drug treatment, may improve outcomes for psychotic symptoms in acute psychosis, including first-episode schizophrenia.

TABLE 10.3

Components of cognitive–behavior therapy in schizophrenia

Cognitive components

- Identifying links between thoughts, emotions and behaviors
- Identifying automatic thoughts
- Hypothesis testing about abnormal beliefs; reframing attributions
- Identifying and enhancing coping strategies

Behavioral elements

- Symptom monitoring; use of diary
- Distraction techniques; focusing strategies for 'voices'
- Graded task assignment
- Anxiety management and relaxation techniques

Improving adherence to medication

Poor compliance with, or adherence to, drug treatment is not unique to schizophrenia. Reasons for non-adherence to antipsychotic drugs are given in Table 10.4. Psychological approaches can improve adherence to medication. Education and explanation about the precise benefits and risks of drug treatment in individual cases should be the starting point, establishing a collaborative approach. This has been taken further using techniques of 'motivational interviewing' borrowed from the treatment of substance misuse. The patient is helped to review what they have to gain or lose by not accepting treatment and remaining or becoming ill. The clinician helps the patient to generate a series of possible options, of which taking drug treatment is one, and to look at the consequences of each. New-generation drugs will further enhance this technique by virtue of their better tolerability.

TABLE 10.4

Contributors to antipsychotic drug non-adherence

- Side-effects, particularly EPS, weight gain and sexual dysfunction
- Perceived lack of efficacy
- Inadequate information
- Complex prescribing regimens
- Stigma
- Delusional beliefs
- Lack of insight

Cognitive remediation

Neuropsychological impairments have been shown to be strong predictors of outcome. Cognitive remediation in chronic schizophrenia aims to train up patients on specific neuropsychological tasks. Recent trials have shown this to be effective and that the gains may generalize into wider aspects of social functioning.

Psychosocial interventions and non-drug treatments – Key points

- Family interventions are known to be effective in reducing relapse.
- Cognitive–behavior therapy in addition to drug treatment reduces persistent positive symptoms.
- Motivational intervention techniques can reduce street drug use and enhance treatment compliance.
- Cognitive remediation reduces some cognitive deficits in chronic schizophrenia.

Key references

Lewis SW, Tarrier N, Haddock G et al. A multicentre, randomised controlled trial of cognitive-behaviour therapy in early schizophrenia: acute phase outcomes. *Br J Psychiatry* 2002;in press.

McFarlane WR, Lukens E, Link B et al. Multiple-family groups and psychoeducation in the treatment of schizophrenia. *Arch Gen Psychiatry* 1995;52(8):679–87.

Meuser KT, Berenbaum H. Psychodynamic treatment of schizophrenia. Is there a future? *Psychol Med* 1990;20:253–62.

Sensky T, Turkington D, Kingdon D et al. A randomized controlled trial of cognitive-behavioral therapy for persistent symptoms in schizophrenia. *Arch Gen Psychiatry* 2000;57:165–73.

Tarrier N, Barrowclough C, Porceddu K, Fitzpatrick E. The Salford family intervention project: relapse rates of schizophrenia at five and eight years. *Br J Psychiatry* 1994;165:829–32.

Tarrier N, Beckett R, Harwood S et al. A trial of two cognitive behavioural methods of treating drug resistant residual psychotic symptoms in schizophrenic patients: I. Outcome. *Br J Psychiatry* 1993;162:524–33.

First episodes of schizophrenia often go undetected and untreated for long periods of time. The median duration of positive psychotic symptoms before detection is 12–24 weeks, but in many cases symptoms endure for much longer before detection, particularly if negative symptoms are taken into account. The duration of untreated psychosis (DUP) is probably the strongest single predictor of response to treatment and of speed to remission in the first episode, although it is not a good predictor of subsequent time to relapse. This observation is the main impetus behind the increasing focus on early detection and treatment of the first episode of schizophrenia.

Early detection

There are two linked questions. First, is it possible to detect, and so treat, people earlier in their first episode? Second, if so, will earlier treatment lead to better outcomes?

The answer to the first question is almost certainly yes. Some of the reasons for delayed detection are given in Table 11.1. Public education, training of family physicians and youth workers in recognizing early signs, and specialist rapid assessment teams have been shown in pilot early-intervention services to reduce median DUP to 6 weeks, with a concomitant reduction in symptom severity by the time of treatment initiation.

TABLE 11.1

Reasons for long duration of untreated psychosis

- Under-recognition of psychotic symptoms
- Delayed referral to specialist services
- Normal variation in individual health beliefs
- Specific symptoms: social withdrawal, loss of insight
- Ineffective first treatments

TABLE 11.2

Possible reasons for link between long DUP and poor outcome

- More severe symptoms by the time treatment is started
- Active psychosis is neurotoxic through dopaminergic or glutamatergic processes
- Prolonged psychosis causes progressive loss of social frameworks (job, family, etc.)
- Long DUP and poor outcome both result from a third variable, e.g. poor premorbid function

It is likely that earlier treatments lead to a better outcome, but this is technically still unproven. Randomized controlled trials of whole services are being attempted. Only part of the link between long DUP and poor outcome is explained by the fact that a long DUP leads to more severe symptoms by the time treatment is commenced (Table 11.2). One caveat recently highlighted is that impaired premorbid function, known by itself to predict poor outcome, may also lead to long DUP.

Optimal treatment in the first episode

Key elements of an early-intervention strategy are given in Table 11.3. Outcome from the first episode is good in 85% of cases, with remission usually achieved within 3 months. Patients in the first episode are

TABLE 11.3

Key elements of an early-intervention service

- Rapid response and assessment
- Youth-friendly and non-stigmatizing
- Family and caregiver education and support
- Effective psychological treatments
- New-generation antipsychotic drug treatments
- Assertive treatment of refractory symptoms

responsive to relatively low doses of antipsychotic drugs, and treatment should be started with the equivalent of 2 mg haloperidol daily or less. Similarly, first-episode patients are sensitive to the side-effects of drugs, and the new-generation antipsychotics are to be preferred.

Although remission from the first episode is not difficult to achieve, 50% of cases will relapse over the next 2 years and 80% over the next 5 years. With each relapse, about 1 in 6 will not subsequently achieve remission.

Prodromal states: can schizophrenia be prevented?

It is possible to identify in the community individuals who are at very high risk of developing schizophrenia in the near future. Table 11.4 summarizes the descriptions of such cases. Overall, follow-up studies show that 25–50% of these will develop schizophrenia or a related psychotic disorder over the next 12 months. Given effective drug or psychological interventions at this prodromal stage, it may be feasible either to prevent, delay or at least ameliorate subsequent psychosis in such cases. The ethical issues relating to the treatment of individuals who may not go on in any case to develop psychosis need still to be fully explored, but this is one of today's most promising research areas.

TABLE 11.4

Operational definitions of at-risk prodromal states

- First-degree family history of psychosis plus recent functional deterioration
- Schizotypal personality plus recent functional deterioration
- Brief, limited, intermittent (less than 1 week) psychotic symptoms
- Attenuated (below diagnostic threshold) psychotic symptoms

From Yung et al. 1996

Early intervention – Key points

- Duration of untreated psychosis is usually 3–6 months.
- The longer the delay in treatment the worse the clinical outcome.
- Early detection has been shown to be possible.
- New-generation drugs are preferred.
- Treatment of prodromal cases may prevent or delay schizophrenia.

Key references

Drake RJ, Haley C, Akhtar S, Lewis SW. Causes and consequences of duration of untreated psychosis in schizophrenia. *Br J Psychiatry* 2000;177:151–6.

Klosterkotter J, Helmich M, Steinmeyer EM, Schultze-Lutter F. Diagnosing schizophrenia in the initial prodromal phase. *Arch Gen Psychiatry* 2001;58:158–64.

McGorry PD, Yung AR, Phillips LJ et al. A randomised controlled trial of interventions designed to reduce the risk of progression to first episode psychosis in a clinical sample with subthreshold symptoms. *Arch Gen Psychiatry* 2002;in press.

Norman RM, Malla AK. Duration of untreated psychosis: a critical examination of the concept and its importance. *Psychol Med* 2001;31:381–400.

Williams J, Spurlock G, McGuffin P et al. Association between schizophrenia and T102C polymorphism of the $5HT_{2a}$ receptor gene. *Lancet* 1996;347:1294–6.

Yung AR, McGorry PD. McFarlane CA et al. Monitoring and care of young people at incipient risk of psychosis. *Schizophr Bull* 1996;22:283–303.

Useful addresses

Patient support groups and research organizations

Center for Mental Health Services
PO Box 42490,
Washington, DC 20015, USA
phone: 1 800 789 2647
www.mentalhealth.org/

Making Space
46 Allen Street, Warrington,
Cheshire WA2 7JB, UK
phone: 01925 571680
fax: 01925 231402
www.makingspace.co.uk

National Alliance for the Mentally Ill
Colonial Place Three,
2107 Wilson Blvd, Suite 300,
Arlington, VA 22201, USA
phone: 703 524 7600
helpline: 1 800 950 6264
www.nami.org/

National Alliance for Research on Schizophrenia and Depression (NARSAD)
60 Cutter Mill Road, Suite 404,
Great Neck, NY 11021, USA
main phone line: 516 829 0091
phone for research grants
program: 516 829 5576
fax: 516 487 6930
helpline: 1 800 829 8289
info@narsad.org
www.mhsource.com/narsad/

Rethink (The National Schizophrenia Fellowship)
Head Office,
30 Tabernacle Street,
London EC2A 4DD, UK
phone: 020 7330 9100/01
fax: 020 7330 9102
helpline: 020 8974 6814
(10 a.m. to 3 p.m.)
advice@rethink.org
www.nsf.org.uk

Professional associations

American Psychiatric Association
1400 K Street NW,
Washington, DC 20005, USA
phone: 888 357 7924
fax: 202 682 6850
apa@psych.org
www.psych.org/

Center for Psychiatric
Rehabilitation
940 Commonwealth Avenue W,
Boston, MA 02215, USA
phone: 617 353 3549
fax: 617 353 7700
www.bu.edu/cpr/

National Institute of Mental Health
6001 Executive Boulevard,
Rm 8184, MSC 9663,
Bethesda, MD 20892-9663, USA
phone: 301 443 4513
fax: 301 443 4279
www.nimh.nih.gov/

National Mental Health
Association
2001 N Beauregard Street,
12th Floor,
Alexandria, VA 22311, USA
phone: 703 684 7722
fax: 703 684 5968
www.nmha.org/

Index